AUTHOR! AUTHOR!

AUTHOR! AUTHOR!

A selection from *The Author*,

the journal of the Society of Authors

since 1890

edited by Richard Findlater

ff

faber and faber

LONDON · BOSTON

First published in 1984
by Faber and Faber Limited
3 Queen Square London WC1N 3AU

Set by Goodfellow & Egan Ltd Cambridge
Printed in Great Britain by
Redwood Burn Ltd Trowbridge
All rights reserved

British Library Cataloguing in Publication Data

Author! Author!
1. Authorship
I. Findlater, Richard   II. The Author
808'.02'0941   PN145

ISBN 0-571-13377-0
ISBN 0-571-13409-2 Pbk

Library of Congress Cataloguing in Publication Data
Main entry under title:

Author! Author! : extracts from the Author,
the journal of authors since 1890.

1. Authorship – Addresses, essays, lectures.
I. Findlater, Richard, 1921–   . II. Author (London, England : 1890).
III. Author (London, England : 1949)
PN137.A8 1984 808'.025'05 84-13509
ISBN 0-571-13377-0
ISBN 0-571-13409-2 (pbk.)

CONTENTS

MY FRIEND BARABBAS

THE SEARCH FOR PATRONS

PUBLIC RELATIONS

QUESTIONS OF CENSORSHIP

THE ONE NECESSITY

CONTENTS

CRITICS AND REVIEWERS

WARTIME ATTITUDES

TRAVELLING FOR MAUGHAM

THE MAKING OF A NOVEL

PROSPECTS FOR POETS

PROS AND CONS OF EXILE

CHANGING MEDIA

CONTENTS

INTO THE LABYRINTH

DARING THE OLD WALL OF DEATH

ACKNOWLEDGEMENTS

My thanks are due to all those authors who have kindly given permission to quote from their contributions to *The Author*: John Bowen, Malcolm Bradbury, Alan Brownjohn, Anthony Burgess, S.H. Burton, Angela Carter, Michael Frayn, William Golding, James Hanley, Michael Holroyd, Storm Jameson, Paul Jennings, Francis King, Rosamond Lehmann, Doris Lessing, Roger MacDougall, John Mortimer, Peter Porter, J.B. Priestley, Allan Prior, Sir Victor Pritchett, Kathleen Raine, Tom Stoppard, William Trevor, John Wain. For permission to quote from other copyright material I am grateful to Brigid Brophy and Katharine Levey (John Brophy); Evensford Productions Ltd (H.E. Bates); Curtis Brown Ltd, on behalf of the estate of Margaret Kennedy; the trustees of the estate of Nevil Shute Norway; the executors of the estates of Arnold Bennett and H.G. Wells; the National Trust (Rudyard Kipling); A.D. Peters Ltd (Rose Macaulay and L.A.G. Strong); King's College, Cambridge, and the Society of Authors (E.M. Forster); Mrs Elizabeth Al Qadhi (John Strachey); Sir Rupert Hart-Davis (Hugh Walpole); A. M. Heath Ltd (John Keir Cross); Christopher Mann Ltd (Benn W. Levy); David Higham Associates Ltd (Sir Osbert Sitwell and Sir Herbert Read); Macmillan Publishers Ltd (Dame Rebecca West); the Society of Authors (St John Ervine, John Galsworthy, Bernard Shaw). We regret that we have been unable to trace the owners of the copyright in the work of Cecil McGivern,

W.B. Maxwell, Kathleen O'Brien and Henry W. Nevinson.

I am especially grateful to Victor Bonham-Carter and Mark Le Fanu for their help in the preparation of this anthology; and to the Arts Council for helping to make possible its publication.

R.F.

February 1984

FOREWORD

Richard Findlater

THE TRADE JOURNAL which has become known to professional writers throughout the English-reading world as *The Author* was born in London on the threshold of the 1890s and a new era in British authorship. It was, H.G. Wells said, 'an extraordinarily favourable time for new writers', of whom he was a prime example in a new kind. 'Below and above alike there was more opportunity. More public, more publicity, more publishers and more patronage.'[1] More cash, too, and more kudos were available to some. There were new ideas, new forms, new outlets, new audiences – and new problems. There was also a new professional body, the Society of Authors – founded six years earlier – which was persuading writers of widely different vintages, backgrounds, and literary kinds to overcome their occupational isolationism and unite in order to protect their rights, improve their treatment and redefine their status in society. By 1890 the Society had enrolled many members and fought many battles. Its Council included such eminent writers as Sir Edwin Arnold, Edmund Gosse, Rider Haggard, Thomas Hardy and George Meredith. It had Tennyson as its President. Now it needed an official organ. *The Author* met the demand from 15 May 1890, as a sixpenny monthly published from the Society's offices at 4 Portugal Street,

[1] Quoted in *The Social Context of Modern English Literature*, Malcolm Bradbury, 1971. Wells joined the Society in 1895.

15

Lincoln's Inn Fields.[2] It was edited – or, as he preferred to describe his role on the front page, 'conducted' – by Walter Besant (1836–1901). This versatile man of letters – novelist, journalist, critic, social historian, administrator and crusader, knighted in 1895 – was the main creator of *The Author* and its parent society, and he left his mark on both of them.

The arrival of *The Author* – following several abortive attempts a few years earlier to establish a periodical addressed, for the first time, to writers – reflected the fact that by the last decade of Victoria's reign there were more British authors, in aspiration and achievement, than ever before. This happened, to simplify history, because there were more British readers than ever before. Twenty years after the introduction of compulsory education, in an expanding population with rising literacy, an unprecedented demand for print was mushrooming throughout Britain. Cheaper, swifter methods of production developed to satisfy the appetites of a growing mass market. The public for books, newspapers and periodicals was increasingly diversified, and so was the range of their authors, contributors and publishers. The Society's membership – and thus *The Author*'s readership – was open to all those 'who have at any time published work that may fairly entitle them to be described as authors, or those who have been or are at present engaged in journalistic work'. At that time journalism seemed to many, as it did to Besant, 'a branch of the literary profession'. There were more newspapers and magazines than

[2] The publisher of the first twelve issues of *The Author* was A.P. Watt, founder of the firm that bears his name today. According to James Hepburn (*The Author's Empty Purse*, 1968) he was 'not the first agent, as has been long supposed, but he was the first person with any sort of public reputation to undertake such work systematically, and for a good many years he was the only one'. His clients included Walter Besant, editor of *The Author*. In 1891, according to Victor Bonham-Carter (*Authors by Profession*, 1978), all *Author* business was transferred to Eyre & Spottiswoode.

ever before: by 1890 their numbers quadrupled compared with half a century earlier, and continued to rise during the decade. Much of the national and provincial press welcomed fiction, essays, reviews and *feuilletons* by members of that still-thriving species, the Men of Letters; while the denizens of 'New Grub Street', as George Gissing called it, helped to fill the columns of the halfpenny press and the shelves of railway bookstalls.

Many more new books were published, year by year: about five times more, by 1900, than the average in the first half of the century (between 1816 and 1851). The total of new novels rose from under 400 in 1870 to nearly 1,000 in 1886, and this figure was almost doubled by the end of the nineties. By then Britain's novels were much shorter and much cheaper: the guinea-and-a-half three-volume mammoths that had dominated Victorian publishing were finally doomed in 1894 when they were rejected by Mudie's and the other circulating libraries. Thenceforth most fiction was published in single six-shilling volumes. When *The Author* was launched, however, the royalty system of paying book-writers was still unknown to most authors, who sold their books outright for a fixed sum (Gissing's *New Grub Street* fetched £150); or published them on 'half profits' (although the total profits were, as *The Author* often protested, frequently kept secret by dishonest publishers); or published them 'on commission', paying all production and promotion costs (as Besant published *his* first novel, written with James Rice). In the year after *The Author* began, 75 per cent of all novels were still published on terms requiring payment by their authors.[3] Nine years later the Net Book Agreement made a new deal possible by regulating and fixing retail prices, thus providing a firm basis for paying royalties.

In the theatre of the 1890s many writers still accepted

[3] This figure was given by Squire Sprigge, Secretary of the Society of Authors 1889–92, and Chairman of the Committee of Management 1911–12.

17

outright payment, although the royalty system had been introduced thirty years earlier (by Dion Boucicault). Eugène Scribe had led the way in France forty years before that. The chronic underpayment of playwrights could not long survive the rapid growth of the entertainment industry. As play-houses multiplied in the capital and throughout the country, as long West End runs were followed by long provincial tours, authors secured their share of the takings; and this may be estimated as one important factor in the renewed vitality of playwriting at the turn of the century, which seemed then to amount to a dramatic renaissance. The Society of Authors, which was joined by 'virtually all the leading playwrights', set up a 'dramatic subcommittee' in 1897. Bernard Shaw, who joined that year, became one of the Society's most active and influential members, as *The Author*'s columns illustrate; although his theatrical cam-paigns – against the censorship and for the national theatre – are reflected less vividly and directly than his polemics against publishers and literary agents.

By the 1890s there was more money to be made from writing, for print and performance, than ever before. The swelling army of authors marching hopefully towards fame and fortune was met by a growing band of speculators, entrepreneurs, publicists, promoters, cultural hucksters and dilettante impresarios, mixed with some sharks and con-men. The commercialization of authorship necessarily ex-posed British writers of all kinds more frequently and more vulnerably to unfamiliar market forces, for better or for worse. To H.G. Wells the literary life seemed 'one of the modern forms of adventure'; to a poet like John Davidson the nineties presented a very different aspect ('nine-tenths of my time, or that which is more precious, have been wasted on the endeavour to earn a livelihood').[4] Through the

---

[4] Quoted in *The Social Context of Modern English Literature*, Malcolm Bradbury, 1971.

Society, *The Author* was founded to help all 'helpable authors' (in Edmund Gosse's phrase),[5] both the 'failure' and the 'successes', to a clearer understanding of their trade – and their trade association.

Like many periodicals it started by promising more than it could ever fulfil. In his opening editorial Besant explained that the organ of the Society was also intended to be 'the organ of literary men and women of all kinds', and that it was to become 'a public record of transactions conducted in the interests of literature, which have hitherto been secret, lost and hidden for the want of such an organ'. He announced, furthermore, that *The Author* was going to be 'the one paper which will fully review, discuss and ventilate all questions connected with the profession of literature in all its branches'. This was an audacious declaration of intent, especially when it is considered in the light of his unusually eclectic view (expressed two years earlier) of what 'literature' really meant: 'the whole of current printed work – good and bad – the whole production of the day'. With so vast a prospectus, how could *The Author* hope to succeed?

No magazines concerned with authorship (a bare half-dozen to date) had as yet survived for more than half a dozen issues. Besant promised twelve issues, 'at least'. He had, it is true, a captive audience. Yet although the Society's membership had increased tenfold since its foundation in 1884 the total was still under 670 when *The Author* was launched. This amounted to little more than 11 per cent of the 'authors, writers and editors' counted by the 1891 census, and less than 3 per cent of the total whom Besant estimated to be 'engaged more or less in literary activity'. Among the 'more or less' literary people who had not yet joined the Society there persisted a stubborn objection to its existence, to the very notion of collective action, and to the

---

[5] His piece, 'The Helpable Author' – from *Grievances of Authors* – appeared in the first issue of *The Author*.

practicality of its aims. This resistance was influenced by what Besant called the 'ridiculous, senseless and baseless feeling' that it was beneath an author's dignity to seem concerned about the marketing, protection and remuneration of his work.

For its first decade *The Author* was, in fact, devoted to the definition and defence of literary property, the prime commitment of the Society itself. Inevitably it was also preoccupied with the reform of domestic copyright and the promotion of international copyright. It strove to expose the exploitation of authors by publishers and editors, and to establish the need for those 'explicit and comprehensive' agreements which, as the American publisher G.H. Putnam said, were unknown in British book business. With these priorities Besant could not fulfil his promise about airing in *The Author* 'all questions connected with the profession of literature in all its branches'. He went on aspiring to give it 'wider aims' and 'a more literary character'. Yet it was, indeed, the limitation of its aims and the concentration of its attention upon the writer's business, undistracted by the seductions of bookish gossip and the skirmishing of literary criticism, that gave *The Author* its especial strength then and during the years to come. Because it was subsidized by the Society it did not have to depend on casual sales or readers' subscriptions: it was sent directly to all members. They were, in fact, frequently urged to pay for it – as many did – and to send donations towards its costs; but these were nominal – 'an estimated £6 per issue' (i.e., 6 annual subscriptions) – compared with the 1983 figure of £2,000 an issue (approximately 400 annual subscriptions). During the first ten years Besant wrote a great deal of *The Author* himself, and for many years, we regret to report, contributors were unpaid.

Walter Besant said, of the Society's abortive predecessor in the 1840s, 'There is one thing, and one thing only, for which those who write books and papers which are sold can possibly unite – viz. their material interests.'[6] He no doubt underrated authors' readiness to rank among those interests such larger concerns as the defence of freedom, even when their own liberties are not directly under threat. Yet it seems clear that the survival and continuing impact of *The Author* was largely due to its service of the author's 'material interests' as part of the Society's programme of professional advice, enlightenment and propaganda. It came at just the right time in history, when writers were being plunged into a confusing and unpredictable turmoil of social, economic and technical change; and Walter Besant was just the right man to run it through its first turbulent decade. With the public prestige and authority of an eminent Victorian all-rounder he combined an exceptional popularity among many of his fellow authors, who responded to his generosity of spirit, his unchallengeable integrity and altruism, and the journalistic zest and courage of his campaigning.[7] Sir Walter set *The Author*'s course to the future. By continuing through succeeding generations to define and champion the rights of authors, to examine their contracts, monitor their treatment and advise them on their professional problems, while acting as a mirror of experience and a forum of ideas about their trade, *The Author* came to occupy a unique place in the annals of twentieth-century writing in Britain.

After Sir Walter's death in 1901 it was edited under his shadow for nearly thirty years by George Herbert Thring (1859–1941), Secretary of the Society of Authors since 1892. A solicitor by profession, nephew of a Law Lord who was

[6] *Essays and Historiettes*, 1891.

[7] Another ingredient of his success was, perhaps, a tinge of paranoia. As he said in an 1897 circular to the Society's Committee from his Hampstead home: 'I submit again, as proof positive that *The Author* is doing great good, the fact that many persons concerned are continually denouncing the paper, showing that they regard it as a paper of the greatest importance, and that they read it with the greatest jealousy; and are either crying out that its facts are not true, or, if they cannot do that, are scheming and working underhand for its suppression or alteration.'

among the champions of copyright reform, Thring was – according to Bernard Shaw – 'far too combative *contra mundum* to succeed in legal practice. . . . He was just what the Society needed then.' (See page 38.) As an editor he lacked Besant's fizz and flair. During his first twenty years in the job he took a narrower view than his rumbustious predecessor of the journal's function, potential range, and justifiable cost. Yet although Thring was no journalist he edited *The Author* with the concern and commonsense that he brought to his secretaryship of the Society, and he used it not only to serve the Society's members but also – at times, and as best he could – to promote the interests of authors at large in the tradition of Sir Walter, whose name remained prominently displayed on the journal's cover as its founding father.

As the Society grew, so did the circulation and influence of its organ; and *The Author* did much to assist the continuing growth of its parent institution, which had increased its membership to 2,500 by the outbreak of World War I. It continued as a monthly – to be precise, there were ten issues a year from October 1901 – until 1917, when under wartime pressures it was reduced to bi-monthly publication. Two years later, in July 1919, it became a quarterly, and a quarterly it has remained. From then on Thring broadened its scope to include more personal and polemical contributions; in October 1926 its title was changed to *The Author, Playwright and Composer*; but it was not until October 1929 that it was given a new look and a new price. After nearly forty years it went up to a shilling, and Sir Walter's name was at last dropped from the cover.

This prefigured changes in the Society itself. In the following year *The Author* announced that Thring (then over seventy) had been succeeded as both Secretary of the Society and editor of its journal by Denys Kilham Roberts, then twenty-seven, who had joined the Society two years earlier as Thring's assistant. Under the convivial direction of this former barrister, who showed a flair for editing which later extended to several anthologies, *The Author* gained more pages, wider horizons, and an often starrier cast of contributors than in Thring's long reign. After twenty-six years Denys Kilham Roberts, while remaining the Society's Secretary General (as the job had been renamed), recruited as his successor on *The Author* and its first 'outside' editor C.R. Hewitt, better known as C.H. Rolph. He was followed in 1961 by the author of this foreword: still in place, he is the fifth editor in ninety-four years. During his editorship the shape of *The Author* has changed twice, its size has risen from sixteen to thirty-two pages, and its cover price has soared from two shillings to two pounds. For the last twenty years it has been printed by one London firm, the Furnival Press.

Since I was first given the privilege and pleasure of editing *The Author* – at the invitation of the Society's General Secretary, Elizabeth Barber – I have somehow committed myself to several impossible tasks, including the attempt to answer in pamphlet form such questions as 'What Are Writers Worth?' and 'The Book Writers – Who Are They?' None has seemed more awesomely incapable of fulfilment than the bid to anthologize ninety years of *The Author* into not many more words than the contents of 2 issues – 1984 size – out of more than 560. But here, by way of introduction, is an exercise of comparable rashness – a summary survey of several conspicuous trends in the trade of writing, and some changes in the worlds of British authorship, between 1890 and 1984.

During the first sixty years of *The Author*'s life more British writers than ever before, or since, were able to live by authorship alone. Beneath this extended but still tiny élite – mainly comprising novelists, dramatists and authors of text-books – was an unprecedentedly large stratum of people for whom authorship was a primary occupation (measuring it by *activity* rather than by *income*). Until the outbreak of World War II and the ensuing social changes many writers had small private incomes which helped them to live without taking salaried jobs. The costs of a full-time writing life, in relation to possible earnings, were much lower than they are today. Jobs were still available in such traditional channels as the Church, the Law and the Civil Service which gave authors, in addition to a regular income, time enough for private writing (although then as now, no doubt, the majority could not believe that they ever had sufficient time or money). There were many more outlets for literary journalism – 'middles', essays, reviews – in newspapers and periodicals that have now disappeared or have largely abandoned such modes of writing and the employment of freelance belletrists. The press market for fiction, too, was much bigger up to 1939. Forty years earlier Besant could say that 'no other kind of work was more in demand', from newspapers as well as periodicals, than the short story: a complete reversal of the situation today. As late as 1922, for instance, thirteen new magazines were launched which published 'a substantial proportion' of fiction, and twenty-seven 'fiction magazines' thrived; none of them survived until the Society's centenary year. Far fewer book titles were published between the wars, compared with the early 1980s; but these had, on balance, a greater chance of being reviewed and even sold. For the authors at the top, royalty scales were higher; a minimum sale for many novels was virtually guaranteed by the commercial lending libraries, on their different levels, supplemented by the public library service; sales in cheap hardback editions and even collected editions continued long after publication, when publishers could afford to keep books in print on their backlist for years. The most successful book writers and dramatists could keep far more of the small fortunes they made than their counterparts can do today, although 1984 top earners

24

may be credited with sums considerably higher in their pre-tax face value. Authors in general enjoyed relatively greater security, more continuity and a somewhat more elevated status than in Victorian times (excluding a handful of eminences) or after 1950. They were ranked by the census near the summit of society, in class 1, until 1961, when they were pushed down to class 2 among actors and musicians (promoted from class 3). (By 1981 authors and journalists were 'socio-economic group' 3, although their 'social class' rating was 2.) In spite of apparent advantages in economic freedom – low-cost travel, for instance – writers' intellectual freedom was restricted by official and unofficial censorship (notably in the theatre) and by the endemic philistinism and puritanism of public taste. Many writers continued to suffer at the hands of editors, publishers and managers from the kind of anomalies, stupidities and injustices against which Besant had struggled in the 1890s.

Looking back from 1984 to *The Author*'s early years across the changing landscape of professional authorship, one may see, among other significant transformations, the impact of 'the paperback revolution', dating from the birth of Penguin in 1936 but not fully apparent until the 1950s. Paperbacks have became increasingly recognized as the main commodity of British booksellers and as the likely basis, in due course, of British publishing. This trend has urgent implications for the future of minority writing whose readership, on past and present evidence, falls dangerously far below the minimum paying audience demanded by paperback economics; and, as things are, this applies to the majority of hardback titles published every year. Yet as most authors agree, far too many of these are published – eight times more than in Besant's day – and the annual total (of which paperback 'originals' form a tiny but growing fraction) is continuing to rise from year to year. The proportion of fiction, however, is declining: from 30 per cent of the total in 1900 (6,000) to less than 11 per cent in 1982 (48,000).

25

Publishing turnover has soared spectacularly – from £10 million in 1939 to more than £1,000 million in 1982 – but the main increase (discounting inflationary factors) has been in sales abroad – from which 'general' authors derive little financial return, compared with home sales – and in the market for educational, scientific and technical books. At home an expanding majority of hardbacks is sold to book clubs, libraries, universities and other institutional buyers who do their business outside Britain's contracting and beleaguered bookshops, whose profit margins are notoriously wafer thin. Year by year more books compete for less shop space: a trend that has helped in the drastic reduction of shelf and storage life for all books, now increasingly disposable, and has thus helped to depress not only the economic status but the vocational satisfaction of their authors. The popularity of borrowing rather than buying books has been a fact of increasing importance in the lives of writers as well as booksellers. Mudie's, which still flourished when the Society of Authors was founded, was followed in the service of a growing middle-class minority by the national chains of Smith's and Boots, and in the 1930s by the 'two-penny libraries' at the lower end of the social scale. From the 1920s onwards these private libraries were increasingly supplemented by the public libraries, which took over in the 1960s when the commercial trade collapsed. By 1970 books were being borrowed from public libraries at the rate of 500 million 'issues' a year: this has now increased to nearly 650 million. This led to the prolonged post-war fight for recognition of the author's 'lending right', first signalled by John Brophy in 1951 (see page 74) and eventually implemented, in a very different form, in 1984.

Other changes in the writer's world during the past century include the post-war growth of state and civic patronage for the arts: this has had decisive results for the theatre and theatre writers, although aid for authorship in print came belatedly, reluctantly and on a tiny, restrictive

scale, which still persists. The abolition of theatrical censorship, as exercised through the Lord Chamberlain's licensing
powers (see page 169), has been accompanied for all authors
by a spasmodic increase in freedoms of language, form and
subject. The comparative loss of economic freedom caused
by the evaporation of private incomes and sinecures in the
Church, Civil Service and other traditional support systems
has obliged many more writers to take full-time non-writing
jobs – in journalism, television, advertising, public relations,
schools and universities. From the author's viewpoint the
newspaper press has shown a growing trivialization and
retreat from literary journalism. The number of periodicals
has continued to increase (between 1970 and 1980 alone by
about 30 per cent), and the most popular – *Radio Times, TV
Times* and the leading women's journals – sell by the million;
but far fewer offer space, at reasonable rates of payment, to
poets, novelists, short-story writers and critics, and the
circulation of the few survivors – many depending on Arts
Council aid – has plummeted in the last twenty years.
Freelance popularizers and men of letters have been ousted
by staff journalists, ghosted celebrities and what Malcolm
Bradbury calls 'the critical salariat', largely based on universities. The closure of *John O'London's Weekly* marked the
end of what V.S. Pritchett described as 'the last attempt to
popularize bookish habits among the self-taught' – among
periodicals, at least. That role has been shouldered, in part,
by television programmes – and the Book Marketing Council.

The principal change in British authorship since *The
Author* started is a phenomenon of the last thirty years: the
radical reduction in the importance of *print* as the main
channel for writers, and the global extension of their potential audience through other media. Already in the 1890s
Besant predicted the emergence of an enormous English-
reading public, estimated at 100 million people. What he
did not foresee was that an even bigger multitude would
come within the reach of British writers through films,

television, radio, video and computers in the still-expanding leisure and entertainment industries serving mass markets. It is a common fallacy that all media are open to a really good writer, that if you can write a book you can work in any other form. Many kinds of book writing are unmarketable outside hard and even paper covers, and only a handful of professionals are all-purpose performers in the cinema, television, theatre, radio, books and journalism. Print remains, necessarily, the major channel for many authors. Yet the flowering of alternative means of expression, the consequent erosion of class-cultural barriers at home, and the growth of an international audience for all kinds of writing have helped all sorts of authors.

Increasing specialization, observable since the 1950s, has been reflected in the growth of the Society of Authors' satellite groups. Translators, radio writers, educational and children's authors have been joined in recent years under the Society's umbrella by medical and 'trade and technical' writers. For the Society these have helped to balance the disappearance of ageing, non-specialist writers who have lost their markets and their resolution to make economic sense out of an increasingly uneconomic activity. Many playwrights of the new generation have a trade union of their own. Television and film writers belong to the Writers' Guild (originally called the Screenwriters' Association, founded in 1937 as a semi-autonomous satellite of the Society), although this organization includes authors who work frequently in print, just as the Society includes those who work frequently in television and other media. Many journalists who might, in Besant's day, have joined the Society are members of the National Union of Journalists. Motoring writers, crime writers, travel writers, science and romance writers all have their own associations, though a large number also belong to the Society. More than ever before the Society reflects its founder's view of its natural constituency as extending beyond poets, essayists, novelists and critics to writers of almost every kind, although it is still predominantly an association of book writers. Economic pressures and the consciousness of common dangers, injustices and anomalies are pushing authors towards a keener sense of professional community and an acquiescence in the possible need for collective action, as may be seen in the mounting militancy of the campaign for Public Lending Right in the 1970s; the vote by a majority of the Society's members in 1978 that their organization should become a trade union; and the current eagerness among members of both major writers' unions for closer collaboration and even formal union.[8]

To use Malcolm Bradbury's terms, 'professionalization' has been accompanied by 'socialization' on an unprecedented scale, frequently subsidized from public funds. This includes the spread of writers' tours in schools or around regional areas, under the auspices of the Arts Council or regional arts associations; the phenomenon of 'writers in residence' at universities, libraries and arts centres; the attachment of playwrights to theatre companies; the submission of books for a proliferation of prizes, almost all unknown before the war; the incidence of writers' conferences, sometimes as a part of festivals; the acceptance by many authors, especially in the theatre, of direct help from the state; the increasing participation of writers in television programmes and in promotional tours. The marketing of books demands, more than ever before, the marketing of personalities. Indeed, another polysyllabic trend – theatricalization – might well be added to those identified above: the

---

[8] It is difficult to give a precise figure for the number of authors in Britain. In 1983, 7,750 book writers registered for Public Lending Right; but a more accurate estimate of the professional writing population may be gleaned from the fact that the Society of Authors, the Writers' Guild and the Theatre Writers' Union together comprise about 4,700 members (with some overlapping); and that about the same number is said to be represented by agents.

writer is increasingly expected to be a performer – as soloist, panellist or interviewee – on television, on radio or in print.

During its ninety-four years *The Author* has remained, as in Besant's day, deliberately limited in its editorial range. It began with a somewhat oversimplified view of publishing, and maintained for many years a dogged hostility to agents; for long stretches of its life (especially under G.H. Thring's direction) it was unduly insular and even parochial; and it sometimes seemed excessively timorous in, for instance, its between-wars hesitations about attacking the absurdities of the 'obscenity laws' and the Lord Chamberlain's stranglehold on the drama. As the organ of a professional society, however, it could not take – and can never take – a completely independent editorial course. It must respect the members' views, expressed by the elected Committee of Management, who decide the policy of *The Author* as well as that of the Society. This Committee is its pacemaker and its invigilator, but not its creator or censor: the journal's contents – happy accidents apart – are planned by the editor in collaboration with the General Secretary and his or her principal aides, a process which for the past twenty-three years has seemed, to the editor, a perfect arrangement.

Now, as for most of its past life, *The Author* is not engaged in publishing original stories and poems (Besant sometimes did, but the stories were usually cautionary tales about wicked publishers or editors and their author victims); it does not commission profiles or assessments of writers, past or present, nor does it attempt to chart literary fashions or discuss sects and covens of writing. Literary value judgements at large are outside the editor's brief, to the editor's relief. As in the past, *The Author* reviews no more than a handful of books during the year, and these are, as a rule, concerned only with the writer's trade. Sometimes it draws attention to memoirs, biographical studies and historical works which contain anecdotes and reflections relevant to the joys and agonies of professional authorship, as well as its contracts and copyrights. It is the miseries rather than the splendours that are, perhaps, most apparent. In many issues there is little sign that, to quote Malcolm Bradbury, 'the independent literary career is a supreme form of the free and uncircumscribed life in our society'. When authors have been disposed to congratulate themselves on their independence or other felicities, it has seldom been in the pages of *The Author*. The journal aspires to be informative, on occasions enlightening, even at times, with luck, entertaining. But its prime concern – now as in Besant's day – is the business and condition of authorship. That concern, together with these mingled aspirations, is illustrated in the following extracts, which show something of the changing dialogue between authors of several kinds and their society, their publics, their publishers, editors, managers and producers, their agents, their reviewers, and their fellow authors.

This anthology does *not* attempt to represent all the major issues and campaigns of the Society. It is a personal choice of personal voices, who will now – with a minimum of compering – be left to speak for themselves as well as their profession and their condition.

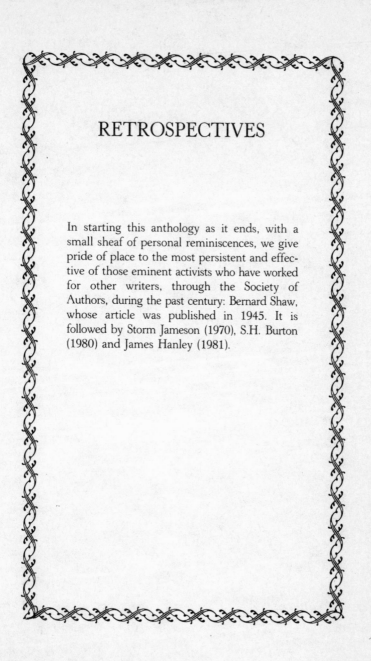

RETROSPECTIVES

In starting this anthology as it ends, with a small sheaf of personal reminiscences, we give pride of place to the most persistent and effective of those eminent activists who have worked for other writers, through the Society of Authors, during the past century: Bernard Shaw, whose article was published in 1945. It is followed by Storm Jameson (1970), S.H. Burton (1980) and James Hanley (1981).

SIXTY YEARS IN BUSINESS
AS AN AUTHOR

Bernard Shaw

I FINISHED MY first book seventy-six years ago. I offered it to every publisher on the English-speaking earth I had ever heard of. Their refusals were unanimous: and it did not get into print until, fifty years later, publishers would publish anything that had my name to it.

It was a novel.[1] Everybody wrote novels then: lucrative literature meant novels and nothing else. Drama, economics and philosophy were unsaleable. William Morris made £100 a year as a poet. Browning, assessed at that figure (at a guess) by the Inland Revenue, left the country. Samuel Butler had to publish at his own expense. Ruskin did the same through a country bookseller, now grown on that foundation into a leading London house.[2] Doughty could hardly get published at all. Publishers and authors lived by novels, novels, novels; and the intellectual heads of the novel-writing profession were George Meredith and George Eliot. When Bryce was over eighty I heard him declare publicly that Tolstoy was 'second only to George Eliot'. Today I must inform the grandchildren of my contemporaries that George Eliot was a woman. But in those days if

---

[1] *Immaturity.* Although it was completed in 1879 – i.e., sixty-six years earlier, not seventy-six – Shaw later revised it twice. He submitted it to ten publishers; the eleventh declined to read it; and it was not published until he included it in his Collected Edition of 1930. (See Shaw's *Collected Letters, 1874–1897*, edited by Dan H. Laurence.) [Ed.]

[2] George Allen & Unwin. [Ed.]

you were an advanced intellectual you read her masterpiece *Middlemarch* or Meredith's *Diana of the Crossways*, for five years' copyright of which he got £500. If you had no such pretension you read Miss Braddon's *Lady Audley's Secret*. Miss Braddon, a very popular romancer, was what we now call a lowbrow; but that epithet had not then been invented. Her style would overawe us now as classical.

When the thirty-shilling market was exhausted the book was reprinted as 'a railway novel' (you were supposed to read it in the train) in yellow boards with a picture on them, price two shillings.[3] It could not be copyrighted in the USA, where, if it sold well, it was 'pirated' by so many competing publishers that the price was run down to ten cents, and the competitors were so nearly ruined that they clamoured for copyright more urgently than the British authors, and eventually got it on condition that they reprinted the book in America to give the American printers a job. But the scalping was so reckless that long after copyright had been established, American editors and publishers, when they asked me to write for them, and I pointed out to them that there are at least a million words of mine in the American public domain freely at their disposal and that I had no time to supply anything fresh, would reply that they dared not touch anything that was not copyright, and that the pressure on my time did not matter, as they would get the articles written and I had only to put my name to them.

The Harper firm, then the leading New York publishers, distinguished itself honourably by sending £10 to every British novelist it 'pirated'. I accepted this gift very gratefully

[3] Michael Sadleir pointed out in a letter published in the following issue that three-deckers 'had an intermediate (and often protracted) run in one volume in cloth, priced at 6s. or 5s. The more popular the story, the longer was the "railway issue" delayed. . . . The yellow-back was not originally synonymous with the "railway novel", but was a subdivision of it; for the earliest "railway novels" were in lettered (or mildy decorated) but not in pictorial boards.' [Ed.]

for the first novel of mine that crossed the Atlantic, but when another firm disregarded my 'authorization' and published a competing edition, I returned the £10. Harper's were so dumbfounded by this scrupulous proceeding on my part that they held themselves bound to give the restored tenner to a charity.

Note that I have put the word 'pirated' between inverted commas. There was no piracy in the matter. If the USA, instead of joining the international copyright convention, preferred to make us a present of their literature and leave us as free to 'pirate' Mark Twain and Artemus Ward (which we did profusely) as they to exploit Trollope and Ouida, the effect being that they could have our books, we theirs, without contributing to the support of the authors, there was nothing dishonest in that arrangement, which still stands between the USSR and the rest of the world, with, however, the important modification that in Russia the foreign author is entitled to a fixed royalty on the sales of his book, and may spend it in Russia. But he may not take it out of Russia.[4]

The establishment of foreign copyright in the USA made an enormous change in the economic possibilities of successful authorship. Dickens, by far the most popular novelist of the nineteenth century, was dismayed by the little he received for the huge success of his *Christmas Carol*, and had to work himself to premature death as a public reader to provide for his large family. He had even to drink himself to death; for his last American tour, which killed him, was achieved only by a diet of fiery cocktails.[5] Were he alive now he could, by holding up his finger, get £30,000 for the film rights of any of his stories in addition to his literary royalties. Even the unorganized literary hacks who still form the bulk

[4] This still persists. [Ed.]

[5] Doris Langley Moore declared in a letter published in the following issue that there was 'not a shred of evidence' for 'this somewhat unkind aspersion'. [Ed.]

of our sweated profession, and who, seventy years ago, toiled in the reading room of the British Museum for eighteen pence an hour, can at least dream of selling a story to Hollywood for the price of a much needed renewal of their wardrobes.

The Reading Room jobbers, being paid on the nail, and never getting as far as having books published, did not dream of trade union organization. Their snobbery would have revolted at the word; and their individual isolation (they were not on speaking terms with one another), to say nothing of their poverty, made organization impossible. But the handful of known authors who wrote books and lived by them were all of Byron's opinion that Barabbas was a publisher. The publishers expected as a matter of course that they should acquire the copyright in the books they published for its whole term; and their favourite agreement was that the author should have half the profits. But their vouchers for the manufacturing expenses, apparently unquestionable, made no mention of the discounts at which they had been settled; and the overhead was not vouched at all. There was virtually a conspiracy of the manufacturers and the publishers to cheat the authors by receipted bills for much larger sums than the publishers actually paid. Occasionally some author would protest and expose this system; but nothing effective was done until Besant began the organization of his profession by the establishment of the Society of Authors, and secured as its Secretary the late Herbert Thring, scion of a legal family, but far too combative *contra mundum* to succeed in ordinary legal practice. He was just what the Society needed then.

Besant, however, was like most authors, no economist. He did not understand publishing as a business. He persisted in assuming that a publisher is an ordinary merchant who, like a baker or dairyman, sells a certain article which everybody can produce with perfect certainty in unlimited quantities, and which everybody needs for use or consumption. He kept on citing quite irrelevant examples of books on which the publisher had made a big profit and the author a little one as damning proofs that the publisher who claims more than the cost of production of the book plus a reasonable profit, say 10 per cent, and does not give all the rest to the author, is a sharper and a robber.

This was an ignorant delusion. Publishing is not ordinary trade: it is gambling. The publisher bets the cost of manufacturing, advertising and circulating a book, plus the overhead of his establishment, against every book he publishes exactly as a turf bookmaker bets against every horse in the race. The author, with his one book, is an owner backing his favourite at the best odds he can get from the competing publishers. Both are gamblers, and must play their game as a game and not as blacksmiths deal in horseshoes and bakers in loaves. Neither has any certainty that the book will sell, yet the extraordinary possibility that, unlike the smith's horseshoe or the baker's loaf, it may be consumed over and over again by generations of readers and be none the worse. Without a single added stroke of work it is possible for the author of a single bestseller, costing six months' easy literary labour, to retire and live comfortably on the proceeds. It is equally possible, and more probable, for the author to spend years of intense labour on the production of a literary work of the highest class, and not make enough money by it to be relieved from the drudgery of reviewing, casual journalism, acting as publishers' reader, and the like bread-and-butter work. Lucrative eminence may come to an author in youth as it did to Dickens, Kipling, and Wells, or never come until after death, as to Blake, Doughty, and Butler. Or it may never come at all.

Trading in such hazards is gambling; and Besant and Thring would have had an easier time if they had understood this and allowed for the fact that a publisher must publish perhaps a hundred books to achieve ten bestsellers. The remaining ninety may barely pay their way, or bring him prestige instead of money, or even flop completely. To keep his shop open he must keep on publishing whether the books he can get are promising or not. That is how the unknown author, the beginner, gets his foot in, as a stopgap, and can get as good terms as an established celebrity because no publisher or theatrical manager will touch the work of a beginner if he can get a book or play by a famous author. And as famous authors are few, and can supply only one book or play a year, whereas the publisher needs at least one book a month, and the manager may at any moment find himself faced with the alternative of finding a new play immediately or closing his theatre if he has one, the authors are often masters of the situation when they know their business well enough to take advantage of it. But they must understand that in gambling there is no question of honest profit and fair dealing. Each side must play 'with all the advantages' and gain on the swings what it loses on the roundabouts. Under such circumstances the wonder is that the publishers do so much to keep up the prestige of literature (properly the business of the State) at their own cost when trash would pay them better. It is by recognizing these conditions and getting rid of the Byron–Besant– Thring tradition that Barabbas was a publisher, that the Society of Authors has become a reasonable body.[6] There are changes still to come which will exercise it pretty severely; but my theme is the past, not the future . . . .

I hardly dare add that the one unchanging factor is the author, socially untrained by his irresponsible solitude and spoilt equally by success or failure, an incorrigible indivi- dualist anarchist, loathing business and its discipline and hating and dreading the few colleagues who know better and drudge at the task of protecting and organizing him. I had ten years of it; and I know.[7]

[6] See 'Confessions of a Benevolent and Highminded Shark' (page 105) for an earlier and rather less tolerant Shavian view of publishers. [Ed.]

[7] In *The Author* of winter 1932 Shaw opened an article entitled 'Mépris de

---

Corps' with the following passage: 'What a heartbreaking job it is trying to combine authors for their own protection! I had ten years of it on the Committee of Management of the Society of Authors; and the first lesson I learned was that when you take the field for the authors you will be safer without a breastplate than without a backplate. They will not combine against the crook publisher and the sweating editor; but they will combine against you and the Society with the fervour of crusaders. They loathe an interfering fellow who, with a soulless eye to business, reminds them that when it comes to selling their work, and incidentally feeding their children, they must come down from romance to vulgar trade unionism and not indulge in splendid gestures at the expense of their profession.'

NOW AND THEN

Storm Jameson

THE MARKETPLACE INTO which an adolescent novelist stepped in 1920 was noticeably emptier and calmer than it is now [in 1970]. I have no statistics to back my conviction, but I am certain that the annual flow of novels was some way below the flood point it reached during the forties and fifties, and from which it is beginning to recede.[1] Even in the restless menaced thirties, the writer's world was a comparatively simple one: the political committees on to which he was drafted and the twinned causes of anti-fascism and anti-war he served (or dodged) were blessedly straight-forward. The cultural structure – a convenient label – was then a scaffolding very poorly provided with ledges for the feet of the young men (and women): if my memory is to be trusted there were few or no societies and organizations waiting to throw down a rope in the shape of grants or awards. But the things a writer desperately needs, elbow room, travel, were easier to come by, and certainly cheaper.

To say that when, in 1945, we emerged as survivors of a civilization, the novelist's world had lost many of its familiar landmarks says nothing. The changes, intellectual and

---

[1] In 1920 8,738 titles were published, of which perhaps a third to a quarter were fiction. In 1937 the total had risen to 17,137, of which 5,097 were fiction. But by 1955 the proportion of fiction had dropped (to 3,702 out of 19,962), and it slumped still further in the following decades until by 1981 it was only 4,747 out of 43,083 titles. Storm Jameson's first novel was *Happy Highway* (1920). [Ed.]

moral, were radical and irreversible. Opportunities, all of them respectable, to make money, a great deal of money, solely *as a writer* – without, that is, being forced to sacrifice time and divert energy to preparing radio scripts or copy for advertisers or . . . complete the list for yourself – proliferated for the young as well as for the older, but not the too old, established writer. On the other hand, the gap separating the careful competent run-of-the-mill novelist from a notable bestseller has today widened to infinity. Today as in 1920 it is possible and very probable that an intelligent and technically competent or modish first novel will earn its author £200 or £300 (worth a fraction of what £200 would have meant to a young novelist in 1920). It is improbable but perfectly possible that it will bring him in £20,000 or more, having by luck or good management broken into the higher circles of the film and paperback worlds. That it may easily be a worthless non-novel about non-persons is irrelevant; the opportunity exists, as in 1920 or 1930 it did not.

If I were starting my career as a novelist now, in 1970 . . . ?

Assume that my ambition is to be a good (intelligent, honest, etc., etc.) writer, not simply the more modest ambition to become the owner of an economically valuable property, an achievement for which I know no absolutely sure recipe. (A quick wit, uninhibited energies, and an astute agent will be of some help.) It will not be enough for me to decide – in all sincerity – that a new theme, masturbation, sadism, sodomy, what you will, best suits a new age. The fact that no subjects are now barred does not make my task easier or my success any more certain. On the contrary. That nothing is taboo, that no political or moral policeman has to be defied or outwitted, may even – it is arguable – account for the curious lack of tension in so much intelligent well-written presentday English fiction, as compared with the novels reaching us from countries where freedom has to be exercised with cunning or bought at a steep price. I do not envy my colleagues in Russia, Hungary, Greece and the

other countries where they prosecute, harry, even kill the
heretic. All I notice is that a lean wolf develops muscles that
a domestic dog rarely needs. It is an uncomfortable thought,
disturbing to our writer's vanity.

But how would I – starting out now and given that I had
not only ambition but a portion of foresight and coolness to
match or balance it – plan my future as a novelist? I hope
sincerely that I would have the sense not to rush into the
wide-open field, but to wait. Not too long, not so long that
the terrible sharpness of young senses – like the sharpness of
sensual excitement which makes a traveller's first moments
in a foreign country worth more to him in insight and
emotion than a year's stay – had lost their acuteness, but
long enough to be able to see myself with a margin of
detachment, long enough, let us say, for me to find the
physical details of copulation neither more nor less interesting and significant than its subtler effects on character – the
first being a matter of common experience and easily
verifiable, where the latter exact great patience and intuition
to uncover – and long enough for my relationships with my
fellow men to begin, at least to begin, to be unclouded by
vanity, diffidence, greed. To wait, say, until my early thirties
before setting about a novel.

I suppose it is conceivable that a Mozart of the novel may
any moment be born knowing so much about human nature
and so much a master of his technique that he has to hurry
to get his work done before dying at an unseasonable age.
Conceivable but, like any miracle, not to be looked for.

I would not – this is important – fill the time of waiting
with any one of the many cultural activities open to an
articulate intelligent young man or woman – journalism,
advertising, the writing of film scripts, poet on the campus,
some comfortable niche in the cultural establishment. These
honourable occupations do not develop the muscles of the
writing mind, they give it what is probably an ineradicable
twist. An exception to this rule is the career, demanding

uncommon perceptions and judgement, of foreign correspondent: any aspirant novelist with the ability to succeed as
a foreign correspondent and the tenacity of purpose to
withdraw when he is still young and malleable enough to
teach himself another use of language will – short of
arranging to be born a genius – have done as well as possible
for himself.

Sooner than become involved in any tempting para-
literary career, I would get myself a thorough training in a
completely different craft – as chef, perhaps, or tool-setter,
or consul, any skill, any profession that I could practise
anywhere, preferably abroad, thus giving myself every
chance to discover the world and human courage, decency,
cruelty, malice, and sparing myself the intolerable anguish
of being forced to succeed, year in year out, as a public
entertainer, spinning my verbal webs, going through my
tricks, perhaps with diminishing intellectual and financial
returns, again and again and again, with the agility of a
street acrobat. It was no talented hack, no industrious
professional novelist who said: 'There is no worse career
than that of a writer who wants to live by his pen. Imagine
yourself forced to produce with your eyes always on a
patron, the public, and to give him not what you like but
what he likes, and heaven knows how exalted and delicate
his taste is. I never forget the tragic faces of a Villiers de
l'Isle Adam, a Verlaine, wearing rags of talent like the
remaining hairs of a moth-eaten old fur. It is indecent to try
to live on your soul, by selling it to the mob.' (Claudel,
writing to a friend from his post in the French consulate in
Prague.)

As a serious-minded novelist who began her trade in
easier years than would face me if I were starting out now, I
say coldly that the habit of writing to pay the bills is
deplorable, pitiable, foolhardy, whatever the ease with which
you invent situations in which characters you have imagined
or stolen from life can show off their sexual and social paces,

their luck or ill-luck, whatever your taste for experiment, however genuine and deeply felt your impulse to expose what is pretentious, shallow, evil, in our doomed civilization, whatever your need to purge yourself of some profound personal crisis, whatever your delight in savage humour, wit, wisdom, and the rest of it. This was always true. Coleridge knew it in 1817 – *'Never pursue literature as a trade.'* It is true an hundredfold now that the novelist is in competition with sacred monsters – television, the film – which can outbid him on every level except the very highest. There is indeed now no level left entirely vacant for him except the one that can be explored only by the writer able to ask, if not to answer, questions it will be no use putting to the most advanced computer, or hoping to have answered in the television studio for the flapping ears of a million listeners.

Starting out now, I would reject the very notion of relying on literature, in any of its forms, in any of its sidelines, for my livelihood. I would count on writing not more than five or six novels in my whole lifetime. I would be prepared to wait at least ten years before attempting to make literature of any knowledge of the world and the human beings struggling in it that I had gathered while serving as tinker, tailor, soldier, sailor – or consul. Even if all I wanted to do was to write about the streets of a mining town, a young man in cracked pointed shoes, the death of a child, or a single incident in a Peruvian village, I would wait until I could do it with scrupulous accuracy. Each of my few books would thus be a *summa mundi*, however infinitesimal the world it created for its readers to move about in. What is more, I should have created it with pleasure and love, without caring a straw about success or failure.

To this, the single advice or friendly warning I care seriously to address to myself at the dawn of my career as a novelist in 1970, I can see only one practical alternative – to have inherited, like Proust, like Tolstoy, an adequate private income.

46

DON'T LET IT GET YOU DOWN: SOME BIRTHDAY THOUGHTS

S.H. Burton

THE BIRTHDAY REFERRED to in the title of this article is not mine. The anniversary that I have in mind is the celebration of the thirtieth birthday of the first book that I wrote. Longman published *The Criticism of Poetry* in 1950, and it's been continuously in print ever since. So this seems an appropriate moment at which to take stock of a long writing life.

I think that I can claim to be an 'average' member of the Society of Authors. I'm a run-of-the-mill pro who has managed to scrape a living by working hard and turning out on time manuscripts made of the specified material and cut to precisely the right length. I've been lucky in that for thirty years I've never been without commissioned work in hand. 'Successes' of the glossy kind – television book programmes, big advances, PRO-managed gravy-train journeys and book-signing sessions – have never come my way. I don't write the kind of books that make the headlines, and anyway I'm not temperamentally suited to being wrapped up in garish packages. I value my independence above everything; and a precarious, hard-won, tenaciously held independence is what my life as my kind of a writer gives me. I've sometimes stayed afloat by being in paid employment (full or part-time), earning in those years far more money for far less work than I've ever earned as a writer. But I've always returned to my freelance life; and I'm there for good (or ill) now.

I have no intention of inflicting a long-drawn-out moan on my readers. I chose the writer's life and I intend to stick to it till death us do part; but there is no doubt that the lot of the professional writer is becoming harder. Both the terms of trade and the conditions of labour are tilting against us.

Inflation has hit many people (though both top people and efficiently unionized labour have escaped its hardest blows) but in one respect it has hit the author harder than anybody else. The sporadic cash flow inseparable from the royalty system was a bugbear when I started. Now, it's an ever-present threat of disaster. Interest rates that keep bankers happy and the pound 'strong' kill authors. An overdraft 'to provide working capital' – in other words, to enable us to buy shelter, food and warmth while we wait for our money – cancels out the 'profits' on a currently earning book, or even two. Surely the time is long overdue for all publishers to pay royalties at least twice a year? I've never been able to see why they can't fork out quarterly. After all, they have a steady inward cash flow from the sales of our books.

Don't imagine that I'm about to launch into a diatribe against publishers. I've published over fifty books with nine different publishers and I'm still on friendly terms with them all – except, of course, for those firms (three out of the nine) swept away by the economic storms through which publishers and authors have lived – or died – since I wrote my first book. I know that authors need publishers and they need successful ones. I rejoice when I read of my publishers' increasing profits. But I do find it necessary to remind them of the old story of the farmer who experimented with an ever-diminishing diet for his donkey. The day on which he achieved the ultimate in economic fodder was the day the donkey died.

The rapid increase in the expenses of authorship has not been balanced by an increase in rewards. A small but picturesque example illustrates this. I used to be able to send handwritten copy to my publishers. (I have a very clear hand.) Now, two copies of a typescript are usually demanded. Publishers' 'Guides to Authors on the Presentation of a Manuscript' read more like Queen's Rules and Regulations or extracts from the Criminal Justice Act than helpful and friendly advice. Penalties for this – sanctions for that – this is not acceptable – that is not allowed – never type more than nine characters per line – allow a nine-line drop for each new section.

The stated reason for these additional burdens on the author is that the meticulous preparation of a typescript keeps costs down and speeds up production. But does it? Not in my experience. Last year, for example, I sent a shortish but rather technical manuscript to a publisher. Because it presented some rather unusual typing problems I paid to have it done. Two copies for the publisher and one for me cost me £60. When the publisher sent me the galleys they were a disgrace – the work of a blundering and illiterate amateur. One chapter alone took me three days to correct, so mangled was the text. When I told the publisher what I thought of the proofs, pointing out that I had sent in a perfect (and expensive) typescript, his reply was: 'Oh, I didn't think they were too bad. They couldn't cope with your technical stuff, I admit, but we had to go to a fairly downmarket firm to reduce production costs. We shan't pay them for correcting their mistakes.' No. And he won't pay me for the extra work that his economies cost me.

No true professional would fail to send in a clear and accurate typescript. It's scurvy treatment to have one's work sent to cutprice printers who aren't up to the job.

Again, there are the ever-lengthening time lags between submitting ideas and sample material and being commissioned, between sending in copy and getting galleys, between sending back galleys and seeing page proofs, between page proofs and publication. We hear a lot about the communications explosion, the introduction of miracle machines into offices, and the speeding up of all 'repro' processes. All I know is that it takes longer to get a book published now than it did thirty years ago. Publishers recruit armies of personnel, but their schedules get longer and longer.

There's still just *one* of me – author, typist (usually), secretary, bookkeeper, filing clerk, post room manager, etc., etc. – and I work faster than I did. Faster and harder. I have to.

At present I have fourteen royalty-earning books in print. Those fourteen books bring me a *gross* income of about £3,000 a year. (My other in-print titles are edited texts for which I received lump sums.) Set off against that kind of income the expenses of authorship (paper, carbons, postage, typing, lighting, heating, books, periodicals, self-employed stamp . . . it would be tedious to fill out a list so well known to you all) and the 'profit' goes whistling down the wind.

I used to supplement the royalties by taking on editorial lump-sum jobs, but I've given that up. The rates offered for such work haven't improved for the last twenty years. Recently, I was asked to prepare an edition of a famous novel by one of our best living writers. The publisher asked for a critical introduction, an analysis of the plot and of the characters, and notes. For all that work he offered £100. I admire that particular author's work very much. I have some small critical reputation of my own to safeguard. To do the job to my own satisfaction I'd have had to spend a month to six weeks on it. So I turned it down. After all, I used to get that kind of fee for that kind of job when I was a beginner.

'Ask for more,' you say? I did. But there's a ready source of blackleg labour in this field. Many a full-time academic will jump at a commission like that for £100 or even less. His name on the cover of a Shakespeare play or a selection of Keats – or any book, come to that – will help him up the next rung of his career ladder. Vanity publishing, as *The Author* pointed out last autumn, takes many forms and it catches a pretty kettle of fish with its varied baits.

When I began my writing life an author with my output in so many different fields – topography, biography, criticism, fiction, anthologies of many kinds, editions of the classics, EFL (English as a Foreign Language) readers, textbooks – would have been making a comfortable living and would certainly not have been forced to work as hard as I know I must.

From June 1978 to May 1979 I worked at a big book for anything up to fourteen hours every day – yes, seven days a week for twelve months. I did spend four days in Stratford, having my batteries charged at the theatre; and I did take Christmas Day and Boxing Day off. Apart from that, I was at my desk at 9 a.m. every day, taking short breaks for meals and an occasional telly programme, finally knocking off only when a numb brain told me that the game was up for the day.

To live, I have to write three books a year, and that's a cracking pace because some of my work is very demanding. My EFL readers, for example, are written within rigid linguistic constraints of vocabulary and grammatical structures. It can be fascinating work but it's very slow. There are days – long ones, too – when 250 words is a difficult target to achieve within that severe discipline.

Don't misunderstand me – I don't think that I'm in any way unusual, either in hours of work or in meagre returns. It's because I think I'm representative of our rank-and-file members that I believe I have the right to describe our lot in our union journal. I've become accustomed to the hard labour and the insecurity. As I wrote at the beginning of this piece I'm prepared to pay a high price for independence and for the chance to practise skills that still give me pleasure. I still get a kick out of this kind of response from a publisher (it refers to a book published a couple of years ago): '. . . thanks to your disciplined writing the book has come out at precisely the 192 pages at which we were aiming.' And the blockbuster that took so much unremitting toil so pleased another publisher that he voluntarily increased the agreed advance because I had 'laboured so far beyond the call of duty'.

As I hope those examples show, I'm not one of the anti-publisher brigade. Some of my best friends . . . ! But I do have to remind them occasionally of what happened to that poor old donkey.

SURVIVING, IN SPITE OF

James Hanley

*At The Author's invitation in 1981 the veteran novelist –
then in his eightieth year – looked back at his writing life
in an article for which he provided the title.*

I ONCE SAID that the writer's real home was on the fringe of
society and that is where I have spent my writing life. I have
never mixed in literary society, belong to no clubs, attend no
popular lunches, and in spite of this I have survived. I have
met only two writers in my life, one of whom was E. M.
Forster. I have spent most of my life locked away in a Welsh
fastness, and there I just went on and on, in my own way,
following no fashion, and not getting unduly depressed by
the periodical, and often depressing, pronouncements about
the death of the novel. . . . 'Once upon a time' still remains
the key to the magic door.

I have probably had more publishers than any other
writer in the country, since I was, after a time, dropped by
one after the other, for I have never been a seller. I can well
understand this, since publishers, too, have to make a living.
I remember having three books issued by one of the best
publishers in London, where I had an allowance of four
pounds a week to keep me going. I sent in my fourth book,
which for me was difficult and challenging, and I have
always liked challenges. I recollect that its first chapter
emerged after about a dozen attempts, and I was well
pleased with the result. Alas, the publisher returned it to

me, and this was the most disappointing part of my career. I was told that *Hollow Sea* [1938] was not up to my level. It must have surprised that publisher to see the novel issued a few months later by somebody else, and indeed it got some splendid reviews.

I have always looked upon books as battles. Even today I never begin a book without being loaded with doubt, and over the course of time it has become my sheet anchor. And I have always loved experiment, especially with dialogue, which was of great help when I came to do an odd play for theatre or television. But I place radio even higher as a medium of communication, where the listener's imagination is always free roving. And I still respect that medium, and have written for it from time to time. The art of radio is creating horizons, and my own experience is that they rarely recede.

What writing has taught me is that an iron will, patience, and discipline are the writer's most important exactments. I learned that with my first novel, *Drift* [1930], where patience itself paid off, though the occasion itself was surprising.

That book made eighteen voyages, from one publisher to another, but I never gave up, and happily its nineteenth trip made a landfall. I might well have called it a day, but I didn't. I still remember the publisher's letter of acceptance, which for me was momentous and exciting, but the surprise for me was the terms of the contract. This contract was written on a single sheet of cheap notepaper, written out in the publisher's own hand. I would, and indeed did, accept the terms. I was paid five pounds outright for the book, with no royalties to follow; moreover I was committed to further books, on the same terms, since the excitement of feeling a printed copy of the novel in my hands was more important than any five-pound note. Before signing this contract I showed it to a friend, on whose advice I sent it off to the then Secretary of the Society of Authors, and I waited for their verdict. This arrived sooner than I expected, and the message

54

that I should have the contract framed, and hang it over my desk, which I didn't do, being too caught up in the pleasure of having the book accepted. It duly appeared, and was very well reviewed, which only increased the pleasure and excitement. I safely anchored this by deciding to go to London to meet the publisher in the flesh. But my interview with him lasted only half an hour, though I left his tiny office in Museum Street five shillings the richer, an unexpected gesture, probably to cover my expenses and perhaps a London lunch.

It was only two years ago that I learned through a bibliographer that the novel had actually gone into two editions in the week of issue, each of 1,000 copies. The publisher in question, no names and no pack drill, actually informed the bibliographer of this, even though he well knew that I myself was still very much around, but about this deception I never heard a word, much less was I approached in the matter. Perhaps one day those long overdue royalties may descend on me, possibly from some new level of the air. But from that moment I knew I was a writer, learned a valuable lesson, and have never forgotten it.

Today I still rejoice over the day I first put pen to paper, and I am as excited about the book I am now working on as I was on my first novel. Its adventures, so well remembered, produce the occasional feel of achievement. Writers just go on writing, since there is nothing else they can do. I was once bearded in my den by a lady who asked me what I was writing about, and all I could say was, 'I don't know, but I will when I've finished it.'

MONEY AND RIGHTS

From the launching of the Society of Authors in 1884 one of Walter Besant's aims was to overcome the insistence of authors as well as of publishers on the secrecy of monetary rewards and the superstitious snobbery that such sordid concerns were beneath the consideration of literary ladies and gentlemen. This leitmotif appeared in Besant's address on the Society's history and progress when he retired from its chairmanship in 1893. We quote below first from the passages selected for publication in *The Author*, January 1893, and then from other writers who have confronted the topic of their rewards and their rights.

I don't want to take up literature in a money-making spirit, or be very anxious about making large profits, but selling it at a loss is another thing altogether, and an amusement I cannot well afford.

Lewis Carroll to his publisher, from Letters to Macmillan, *edited by Simon Nowell-Smith, Macmillan, 1967 (quoted Winter 1980)*

COMMERCIAL VALUES

Walter Besant

THERE HAS EXISTED for 150 years at least, and there still lingers among us, a feeling that it is unworthy the dignity of letters to take any account at all of the commercial or pecuniary side. No one, you will please to remark, has ever thought of reproaching the barrister, the solicitor, the physician, the surgeon, the painter, the sculptor, the actor, the singer, the musician, the composer, the architect, the chemist, the physicist, the engineer, the professor, the teacher, the clergyman, or any other kind of brain worker that one can mention, with taking fees or salaries or money for his work; nor does anyone reproach these men with looking after their fees and getting rich if they can. Nor does anyone suggest that to consider the subject of payment very carefully – to take ordinary precautions against dishonesty – brings discredit on anyone who does so; nor does anyone call that barrister unworthy of the Bar who expects large fees in proportion to his name and his ability; nor does anyone call that painter a tradesman whose price advances with his reputation. I beg you to consider this point very carefully. For the moment any author begins to make practical investigation into the monetary value of the work which he puts upon the market a hundred voices arise, from those of his own craft as well as from those who live by administering his property – voices which cry out upon the sordidness, the meanness, the degradation of turning literature into a trade. We hear, I say, this kind of talk from our own ranks –

59

though, one must own, chiefly from those who never had an opportunity of discovering what literary property means.

Does, I ask, this cry mean anything at all? Well: first of all, it manifestly means a confusion of ideas. There are two values of literary work – distinct, separate . . . they cannot be considered together. The one is the literary value of a work – its artistic, poetic, dramatic value. . . . On that is based the real position of every writer in his own generation, and the estimate of him, should he survive, for generations to follow. I do not greatly blame those who cry out upon the connection of literature with trade: they are jealous, and rightly jealous, for the honour of letters. We will acknowledge so much. But the confusion lies in not understanding that every man who takes money for whatever he makes or does may be regarded – not offensively – as a tradesman; that the making of a thing need have nothing whatever to do with the price it will command; and that this price in the case of a book cannot be measured by the literary or artistic value.

In other words, while an artist is at work upon a poem, a drama, or a romance, this aspect of his work, and this alone, is in his mind, otherwise his work would be naught. But, once finished and ready for production, then comes in the other value – the commercial value, which is a distinct thing. Here the artist ceases and the man of business begins. Either the man of business begins at this point or the next steps of that artist infallibly bring him to disaster, or at least the partial loss of that commercial value. Remember that any man who has to sell a thing must make himself acquainted with its value, or he will be – what? Call it what you please – overreached, deluded, cheated. That is a recognized rule in every other kind of business. Let us do our best to make it recognized in our own. . . .

Sir Walter Scott did not despise the income which he made by his books; nor did Byron; nor did Dickens, Thackeray, George Eliot, Charles Reade, Wilkie Collins, Macaulay – nor, in fact, any single man or woman in the history of letters who has ever succeeded. This pretended contempt, then, does it belong to those who have not succeeded? It is sometimes assumed by them; more often one finds it in articles written for certain papers by sentimental ladies who are not authors. Wherever it is found, it is always lingering somewhere – always we come upon this feeling, ridiculous, senseless, and baseless – that it is beneath the dignity of an author to manage his business matters as a man of business should, with the same regard for equity in his agreement, the same resolution to know what is meant by both sides of an agreement, and the same jealousy as to assigning the administration of his property.

• • • •

Authors can't make what I call *money*. . . . They can only make a fair income if they have a great deal to say – like Shaw, Wells and me – and are incurably industrious, as we are. And they can only make it even then by not trying to make it. . . . Withal, thanks to agents and Authors' Society, the economic position of authors has greatly improved in my time.

Arnold Bennett, in a 1925 letter to Lord Beaverbrook, from *Letters of Arnold Bennett*, vol. 3, Oxford University Press, 1970 (quoted Autumn 1970)

BENNETT v. WELLS

It was not until The Author *had been going as a monthly for about a year that a correspondence column became established. At first the majority of letters were signed by such pseudonyms as 'Pachyderm', 'Rossignol', 'Ignotus', 'No Pay, No Pen' and 'Berserker'. As time went on, and the Society of Authors grew in strength, some of the leading writers of the day sent letters to its journal. These exchanges in 1913 between H.G. Wells and Arnold Bennett were prompted by the following letter from 'Justice':*

Dear *Author*, – An author can exist without publishers. But show me the publisher who exists without authors. I should like to know how much, to a ha'penny, writers like H.G. Wells, Arnold Bennett, or G. Bernard Shaw have put out advertising to arrive at their present stage of success. Wouldn't it be a good plan to have them, for the benefit of the many, divulge the lump sums they have earned *minus* their advertising bills – and their agents' charges?

JUSTICE

Dear Sir, – I am always ready to oblige a fellow member of the Authors' Society, and so let me help 'Justice' to the career he contemplates by telling him that the sum 'to a ha'penny' I have 'put out advertising' to 'arrive' at my 'present stage of success' is just exactly £0 0s 0d, and I have no doubt that Mr Bennett and Mr Shaw will confess to an equal parsimony. What my publisher spends is between himself and God. I never pay for advertisement or corrections, never allow an agency clause in my agreements (I generally don't do business through agents), always take 25 per cent upon a 6s book, always exact a big cheque on account of royalties (rather larger than what is caused by the certain sales), always reserve the right to publish a cheap edition at less than 13d at the end of two years, and never suffer a 13 as 12 clause. I draw up my own agreements with Messrs Macmillan, who also, as a matter of courtesy – and subject, of course, to a considerate use of the privilege – give me unlimited free copies. If an author is really worth while publishing, he can get these terms from any decent publishing house, and I wish we could make some agreement among authors to hold the publishers generally at this level.

In the past I was not so wise as I am now; I left nearly all my business to an agent. I am still encumbered with his slovenly and disadvantageous agreements. Now I do business with an agent when it suits me. None of them is good all round, and none can be trusted to 'handle' the whole of an author's affairs. One agent is rather good with short stories, another is brilliant at a serialization, another who goes about upsetting authors with imperfectly substantiated offers of large sums in order to get hold of their business is a dangerous nuisance.

The ideal thing for an author to do is to fix up a standing agreement on the lines I have given above with a big honest solvent firm, give his books to a capable agent to serialize – and think no more of these things.

H.G. WELLS

Sir, – Can't we beginners in our beloved profession henceforward, to defeat the 'shark' publishers establish a league to be known as the Wells League that has for its ideal agreement the one Mr Wells advises, and for its actual one something just as near it as feasible?

Mr Wells writes: 'The ideal thing for the author to do is to fix up a standing agreement on the lines I have given above with a big solvent firm – and think no more of these things.'

Did Mr Wells 'think no more of these things' in the days before he, on his own terms, advertised the publishers – gratis?

Won't Mr Wells tell us something of his 'green and salad' experiences with publishers? We can't write as he does. Who can? But Napoleon was no less Napoleon at St Helena than at Corsica, was he? at Waterloo than at Austerlitz.

JUSTICE

Sir, – So long as my friend Wells is content to speak for himself about agents I am ready to listen in respectful silence, but when he begins to speak for 'all sensible authors', I must protest. I maintain that I am a sensible author. If lampoonists and satirists are to be believed, I have a reputation for considerable business acumen. Bluntly, I think this reputation is deserved.

As one 'sensible author', I wish to 'proclaim clearly' that I should not dream of employing agents only 'for specific jobs'. On the contrary I am absolutely convinced that every author of large and varied output ought to put the whole of his affairs into the hands of a good agent, and that every such author who fails to do so loses money by his omission. I admit that some agents are bad. I know that some are good. A good agent will do a specific job better than an author, partly because he knows the markets better, and partly because he is an expert in the diplomacy of bargains. But a good agent is also very valuable in utilizing opportunities as they arise – opportunities of whose very existence the author is ignorant. I reckon that in the latter activity alone a good agent recoups an author again and again for the whole of his commission.

In my experience it is precisely when agents are employed only for 'specific jobs' that trouble comes.

Wells, my senior, once advised – nay, commanded – me to go to an agent. With my usual docility I did so. He told me to put the whole of my affairs into the hands of the agent. I did so. I have never regretted it. I have never had the slightest agency trouble as the result of following Wells's advice. I am quite sure that if I had not followed his advice I should be very decidedly worse off than I am. My gratitude to Wells is lasting. That happened some thirteen years ago. Experience has led Wells to change his views. Experience has only confirmed me in my views, formerly his. He may be right; I may be wrong. I will not dogmatize. But he must not speak for 'all sensible authors'.

ARNOLD BENNETT

I am obliged to the Editor for a sight of E.A.B.'s letter in proof. His fault has ever been modesty. I deplore my forgotten advice. His reputation was already made in those days, his future secure. Without that 'good agent' he must still have had all his present prosperity plus 10 per cent. How are we to prove these things? Shall we sit down together and discuss our translations, our serializations? Details in public would be difficult. I must talk privately to E.A.B. in this connection.

H.G.W.

Dear Sir, – May I say a little more in reply to the second letter of 'Justice' in your last issue? At the risk of seeming obtrusive with my business particulars I feel that with a very little trouble to myself I may be of some real service to the numerous beginner writers who are destined to produce, among other matter, much of the literature of tomorrow.

Then let me relate that I did not begin with books – I could not afford the time. I think that was a very lucky restraint. I had to live, and so *I learned to write before I thought of a book*. I had already made a little reputation, when the time came for dealings with a book publisher. I published three books almost simultaneously. I got 10 per cent for each, and advances of £5 (for a very flimsy little volume of newspaper articles), £50 (for a continuous story published at 1s 6d that had already had a success as a serial), and £20 (for a volume of short stories), respectively. (The short-story volume only was published through an agent.) These are, I think, very fair beginner's terms. A beginner should always demand a cheque on account of royalties as a guarantee of good faith, and a royalty of 10 per cent gives the publisher a very handsome margin of profit. It is no good to the beginner to be greedy about the royalty. I mentioned 25 per cent in my last letter as the ideal for an established writer. What a beginner needs is advertisement and pushful selling, and *that is guaranteed by the cheque on account*. Better for him 10 per cent and £50 down, than 25 per cent and nothing down.

One of these first three books was *The Time Machine*. I had previously refused an invitation from Mr X to undertake part of the expense of publication and trust to him. At times we meet, and I remind him of that incident. He is quite a well-known publisher.

It has been a matter of regret to me that those first three agreements were not limited to a term of years. No just publisher will object to such a limitation upon the part of a beginner – five or seven years is reasonable; and it affords an opportunity for rearrangement if the beginning develops into success.

Also let me assure the beginner that it is particularly ridiculous for *him* to trust to agents. If an agent were your agent *only*, or agent only for you and a select group of authors, there might be some sense in giving over your affairs to him; but every literary agent seems promiscuously disposed to grab 10 per cent of any transaction going, and it is so obviously to every agent's interest to 'keep in' with publishers and so unimportant to them whether they grab their tenths on this man's work or that man's work, that except in the case of very big and conspicuous and valuable authors indeed – and every agent must, of course, be able to claim one or two big authors, commercially speaking, before he can get his chance among the minor crowd – I do not see how any real services can be expected from them. It is just because I see them now taxing the writing public at large on the strength of one or two generously grateful special cases, that I am calling attention to the ordinary facts and the plain commonsense of the agency business. It is not simply that agents need not and do not display any exclusive loyalty to their clients; most of them get the money so easily that they do not even trouble to draw tolerable agreements, save American copyright, secure complete serialization, realize minor rights, or do the most manifest duties of their position. No agent that I have ever heard of can handle translation business, for example, and, indeed, most of the British agents know no language but English. I can speak of only one really efficient agent in London at the present time, and he deals in a speciality, the negotiation of serials. I am told, but I have no sure knowledge, that another understands this new and peculiar cinematograph business. He limits his work as every genuine agent should to a specified list of clients. There may be yet others meritorious, but unknown to me.

I quite agree with 'Justice' that it would be easy to draw up a standard agreement that would cover all the possibilities of most books, and which would be fair to both author and publisher. I think, indeed, this Authors' Society Model Agreement is a little overdue. I should be very pleased to assist in its preparation.

H.G. WELLS

O'BRIEN v. SHAW

In Spring 1931 Bernard Shaw took part in a symposium on the question, 'Has the theatre manager any moral claim to an interest in the film rights?' G.B.S. answered this with a general harangue about authors' imbecilities, published below. In the correspondence columns of the following issue he in turn was harangued by Kathleen O'Brien.

AN AUTHOR WHO gives a manager or publisher any rights in his work except those immediately and specifically required for its publication or performance is for business purposes an imbecile. As 99 per cent of English authors and 100 per cent of American ones are just such imbeciles, managers and publishers make a practice of asking for every right the author possesses: translation rights, world rights, dramatization rights, and film rights for the whole duration of the copyright at a fraction of their market value. Imbeciles are always afraid to say no; and the result is that the concession of such rights soon becomes customary – with the imbeciles. The first time I ever negotiated the London production of one of my plays the acting manager who had been told to settle with me remarked pleasantly, 'Of course you will give us the American rights.' I grinned and replied, 'Of course I won't.' He grinned and dropped the subject. If I had been an imbecile I should have assented nervously.

That is how the thing is done. Authors who have not brains enough to understand their legal and economical position, nor character enough to take care of their own interests, had better put themselves in the hands of the professional association to which they should belong (in Britain the Society of Authors) and allow it to dictate their agreements and collect their royalties. But many authors are not intelligent enough in the real world (they are all perfect Einsteins in the realm of fiction) to join an association; consequently they undersell their more sensible colleagues so disastrously that the professional association finds the market spoilt by the competition of the nerveless and spineless blacklegs who will take anything that is offered to them and grant any concession that is asked. Thus we find the Authors' League of America letting down its members heavily by conceding in its minimum basic agreement half the film proceeds as of right to the theatrical managers: a monstrous and perfectly gratuitous betrayal of its members. Still, it is better for an American imbecile to be let down half-way by the Authors' League than to be let down to the ground by his own greed for production or publication, and his own timidity. In the same way, though it is never worth an agent's while to stand out for the top price which an author of full business competence can obtain for himself, yet for an imbecile it is better to make a middling bargain through an agent than a very bad one without an agent.

Nothing will save the majority of authors from themselves except a ruthlessly tyrannical professional association having no other interest than to keep up the market to its highest practical possibilities. And this is very difficult to establish as long as authors work separately for their own hands (usually hands with no business muscle in them) and never dream of considering the interests of their profession as a whole when they are driving their little bargains with their exploiters, who naturally do most of the driving. It is pitiable to see a body of professional men on whom the Copyright Acts have conferred a monopoly of enormous value unable to do for themselves what is done by porters and colliers and trade unionists generally with no monopoly at all at their backs.

G.B.S.

To compare, as Mr Shaw compares, the position of authors with that of 'porters and colliers and trade unionists generally' is to reveal a disregard of essential differences that gives one a faint glimpse into the horrors of a Shavian Utopia. Porters and colliers are trading in a commodity that the public primarily wants and cannot do without, or can do without only at the cost of supreme discomfort to itself; authors are trading in a commodity that the public does not primarily want, and can forgo with no embarrassment whatever. The public has to be persuaded to want the author's commodity by an expensive and intricate system of suggestion, combining coaxing, bullying and the wearing down of resistance by prolonged repetition, generally called advertising. In the case of the collier, one lump of coal is very like another lump of coal: there is no personal, creative relationship between the man and his product; but in the case of the author every book is a complete and separate entity, and the whole book trade is bound up with this personal factor, complicating the selling of his wares in a way unknown to the simple state of the collier.

To talk as though an obscure author and a battle-scarred publisher fighting over a contract commanded equal weapons and ammunition is nonsense. The publisher has the big guns every time. The author has perhaps sent his novel to half a dozen publishers already, all of whom have rejected it. Allowing the usual average period of three months for the retention of a manuscript that could be read in three days, eighteen months have been lost, during which the author has received not a penny profit on his work. In addition, extreme depression has gradually set in, lowering his morale, impoverishing his vitality, slackening his blood

70

stream, impairing his vibrations, and setting up in his spirit a jaundiced view of the universe generally, all of which has a very material and harmful effect on his productive capacity. The seventh publisher to whom the author sends his manuscript, unexpectedly, as the latter is comparing the rival advantages of the old-fashioned prussic acid and a modern-type gas oven, offers to publish it. He prepares a contract based on terms which are naturally to his own advantage. The author, bracing himself jauntily as a terrier to face a bloodhound, says, 'Nonsense! I can't give you my American, film, dramatic, translation, posthumous, ante-natal and post-millennium rights. Mr Shaw says I shall be an imbecile if I do.' The publisher replies: 'Mr Shaw is probably right. You may be an imbecile, but I'm not. Good morning.'

What is the author to do? Send his book to half a dozen more publishers, wasting another eighteen months, and facing the possibility of its failing to find a publisher in the end? There exists a myth among literary organizations that a really sound, sellable book will always find a publisher sooner or later. There exists another myth that a book that is able to interest one publisher is able to interest another.

The fact is that the intrinsic worth of the book, play or whatever the author is trying to sell is the least, last factor in the whole transaction. There is probably no other trade in which there is so little relationship between profits and actual value, or into which sheer chance so largely enters. Authors, suggests Mr Shaw, being imbeciles, should allow the professional organizations to which they belong to 'dictate their agreements and collect their royalties', showing that the author of a *Saint Joan* does not always reveal the sagacity of a Saint Bernard. How can you 'dictate' an agreement about an article of which there is neither a standard nor as yet even a calculable market value, and of which the sale depends on factors many of which are entirely fortuitous? As though the quality of the book conditioned the terms of the contract, as the quality of the coal conditions its market price! The association might dictate the agreement, but I doubt very much, for obvious reasons, whether it would collect the royalties.

Can the struggling author be blamed for accepting terms, until he is in a position to do otherwise, that he knows perfectly well to be one-sided? The one thing of paramount importance to him is to have his work published with the minimum loss of time. Naturally the publisher, being in a position to do so, exploits the author's necessity, as the author would certainly do to the publisher if their positions were reversed. Once the author has acquired some kind of status in the literary market, once he can reasonably be banked on to command at least a certain minimum sale, he can turn down contracts and accept others with some degree of authority; but to expect a fledgeling author to refuse a contract that might not appeal to Mr Shaw is to ask rather too much of human nature. And there is quite a lot of human nature about authors. Ask authors.

K.O'B.

• • • •

No society, corporate or private, ought to be allowed to purchase a copy of a book and make it the common property of many hundreds of readers. Clearly the author is robbed by such a proceeding. The writer of a modern book ought to be paid a royalty every time a copy of it is lent out of a library – at any rate a public library. In many places it is the *rich* and not the *poor* who make the greatest use of these institutions; and I protest against the meanness which pays a penny for that which ought to cost 6s or 10s. The committee of a library buys two or three copies of a book with a name; and those two or three copies go through the hands of, perhaps, two or three thousand persons, many of whom would buy copies if it were not for the blessed (*blessed* is not exactly what I mean) free library. The readers pay a penny 'towards the expenses'. Why should not each borrower pay

the author another penny? Or those Carnegie chaps ...
might pay it for them; and, of course, pay it with a
handsome margin.

Paul Fountain, July 1909

At a certain seaside circulating library, I paid twopence for
three days' use of a six-shilling novel. From entries therein, I
found that eighty-five other persons had made like payments, making a total of fourteen shillings and fourpence for
the use of a book which was still in active circulation. I also
discovered that the borrowed book was a *review copy*,
evidently purchased by the proprietor of the circulating
library for 'a mere song' from the editor of a newspaper, who
had received it gratis from the publisher.

Usually at least sixty copies of a six-shilling novel are sent
out for review. If only half of these are sold to second-rate
circulating libraries, and each of them is perused by eighty-
six persons, this means that *the author of the book secures
2,580 readers who do not bring a single farthing into his
exchequer.*

In provincial towns I have noticed that the proprietor of a
circulating library is frequently a bookseller, printer, and
editor of a local newspaper. If he can get a six-shilling novel
for nothing, or next to nothing, and make fourteen shillings
and fourpence by lending it to eighty-six persons – as in the
case I have noticed – he 'takes the biscuit' from publisher
and author, and no mistake!

I have long contended that authors might become their
own publishers, and distribute their own books by establish-
ing bookstalls at hotels, as in America, if they had a
sufficiency of co-operative enterprise.

It is simply a case of 'Wake up, Authors!'

Henry J. Swallow, July 1910

73

A PROPOSAL TO INCREASE AUTHORS'
INCOMES THROUGH THE LIBRARIES

John Brophy

*More than thirty years ago, in Summer 1951, John Brophy
initiated a new series, 'Open Letter' – a forum for the expression
of individual points of view – with a scheme to raise writers'
incomes. Although his central proposal, to pay authors a penny
per library loan, was dismissed as financially and politically
impractical by the Public Lending Right campaigners of the
1960s and 1970s (whose leaders included his daughter Brigid),
Brophy's article has an especial interest today.*

LIKE OTHER CITIZENS, the author suffers from rising prices
and heavy taxation, but that is only the beginning of his
troubles. As soon as people discover they have less money to
spend, the source of the author's basic income, book sales,
dwindles rapidly, and now there is a threat of a general
reduction in royalty rates. In this way the author is subjected
to a triple economic compression.

The situation, deteriorating month by month, has never
been one which authors, with a few lucky exceptions, could
regard as satisfactory. The book trade, organized to produce
material volumes and distribute them to the public through
three main 'outlets' – the book shop, the commercial circulating library and the public library – provides a livelihood
and economic security for tens if not hundreds of thousands
of employers and employees. No one would wish it to be
otherwise, but the shocking anomaly remains that the book
trade, which supports printers, binders, publishers, book-

74

sellers and librarians, does not support more than a small minority of authors. Without authors, the book trade could never have come into existence, and without them it would quickly perish, yet I doubt if one author out of ten, among those sufficiently 'established' to have a reputation and a public, earns a living by his books. There may be a few left with a private income but in general the other nine out of the ten keep themselves by taking a job and writing only in their spare time.

I am not going to argue that anyone who elects to call himself or herself an author should be subsidized, but there are two relevant propositions which seem to me beyond dispute. First: it is in the public interest that an author whose work commands the respect of critics and a sub-stantial number of readers should earn enough by it to enable him to go on writing. The second proposition is this: except in his youth, an author cannot use his powers with full intensity in his spare time, after his nervous and physical energy has been used upon other tasks.

Government patronage has been suggested as an aid to young writers, but even if the implications were accepted, it would ameliorate conditions only for a few. There is no prospect of an all-round increase of book sales, and none whatever of increased royalties. Nevertheless, I believe that the lot of all authors can be quickly and radically improved, and earnings substantially increased. The cost would be borne by the people who ought to bear it, the book-reading public. The greater part of that public does not buy books: it borrows them from libraries. A volume in one of those libraries may be read and enjoyed by hundreds of people, but all the author receives is, through the publisher, a percentage royalty on the original sale to the library. It is here, in this important section of the book trade which we all tend to accept on its own terms, that a large untapped source of income for authors is to be found.

Commercial libraries are maintained by period subscriptions paid in advance, and public libraries are subsidized out of the rates – it is a misleading euphemism to call them 'free' libraries. The scheme I am putting forward would in no way alter either of these methods of defraying the cost of stocking and running libraries. The innovation would consist of a borrowing fee to be paid by the reader each time a volume is 'taken out'. The fee I suggest is one penny, and, after certain deductions, it would go wholly to the author of that volume.

The borrowing fee is so small that, although there may be a few grumbles at first, it is inconceivable that the book-borrowing public would not quickly acquire a new habit of handing over one or more pennies on each visit to a library. To publishers and booksellers this new habit would have special advantages: it would set a new value on books and help to break down that traditional contempt of many British people towards a commodity which at present can always be got apparently for nothing. Nor do I believe that there would be any falling off in the turnover of libraries. People want to read books because they provide a personal experience for which neither films, radio nor television is an adequate substitute, and a penny a time will not put them off. The pennies, however, added up, would make a big difference to authors. . . .

The suggestion that it would only be equitable for book-borrowers to pay something to the authors of the books they enjoy was advanced this spring in *W.H. Smith's Trade Circular* by Mr Eric Leyland, who writes books for children, and is therefore unlikely to receive much benefit himself. His altruistic suggestion was vigorously attacked by three librarians and, when I weighed in with a more detailed proposal extending the idea to the public libraries, the discussion was brought to an abrupt end. If the scheme is carried further, strong opposition must be looked for, especially from librarians. It must be foreseen and patiently countered if we are to seize this, the one opportunity of improving the conditions of authorship. Payment by percentage royalties was not established, in place of the older system by which publishers bought up an author's copyright, lock, stock and barrel, without overcoming opposition. The payment of royalties, a welcome reform in its time, no longer provides an adequate income for the majority of authors, whose competence is not otherwise in doubt, and the time has come for it to be supplemented. I suggest that, if the proposal finds favour, the Society of Authors should forthwith, by an *ad hoc* committee or otherwise, address itself to two specific tasks: to draft a practicable scheme of administration and to discover and pursue the best means of carrying the scheme into effect, either by written agreement with the libraries or, if necessary, by Act of Parliament.

I seem to remember a similar suggestion being aired before the war and being dismissed by members of the book trade as impracticable. Fortunately, there is now a precedent to answer that argument [in Denmark] . . . .

Who could seriously complain at paying a penny for the right to read a book when a single cigarette costs twice as much, and the compulsory weekly contribution to National Health and Insurance (from which no benefit may ever be drawn) is 4s 11d for those in employment and 6s 2d for those, including authors, who are classified as 'self-employed'? The borrowing fee should, I think, be specifically known as the Author's Fee, and the public should be told, through the Press and on notices displayed in all libraries, that their pennies are going to keep authors, not in luxury but in reasonable security, so that they can go on writing.

The method of collection could be quite simple. Each penny would be paid over the counter in exchange not only for the book borrowed, but for a numbered ticket of the 'cloakroom' type such as is at present used in public libraries for fines on overdue books. The ticket would serve as a receipt and as a check on the amount of cash taken each day.

All libraries keep a record of book loans either in the back of each volume or in a card index. A deduction of 10 per cent from the total of Author's Fees collected by each library should amply cover the cost of extra bookkeeping, banking and clerical work. The remainder would be paid every six months to the publishers concerned who, after deducting a further 10 per cent to cover their own expenses, would forward the appropriate sum to each author.

There would be exceptions and complications. Anthologies, miscellanies, translations and books written in collaboration would need special treatment. Borrowing fees on 'classics' and other out-of-copyright works, on atlases and books concocted by publishers on which royalties are not paid, might be set aside to form a fund for the benefit of poets and scholars whose books are never printed in large editions. The scheme would involve no hardship whatever for the general public, but the appropriate authorities might be asked to subsidize old age pensioners and students to the extent of, say, 50 or 100 borrowing fees a year.

Opposition may be expected from librarians who will not welcome the necessity of reorganization and extra work, and who will probably demonstrate the normal human reaction to a new idea. We shall be told that the public will give up reading rather than pay a penny a time, and that the conception of the 'free' library is sacrosanct. We shall be told that commercial libraries already make only a small profit and the scheme will endanger even that. . . . We shall be told that libraries already render a great service to authors, especially to young authors, many of whom would not be published at all but for their publisher's reliance on library orders. This is true, but the libraries do it not to please authors but to please their paying customers; the benefit is mutual.

The argument on which the opposition is likely to concentrate, however, is the crucial one. We shall be told that on every volume bought by a library the author already receives a percentage royalty, and for him to ask for further payment is greedy and unreasonable. This argument is not valid because it assumes that only one transaction is involved, the sale of the volume to the library, whereas the library exists to carry out further transactions with the same volume in the form of loans. For each of these loans the library receives payment, either by subscription or by subsidy from the rates, and it is time that the author, on whom the whole system is founded, and who cannot live on his royalties alone, also received payment. A penny a time is not too much to ask.

SOCIAL DILEMMA

Walter Allen

Is THE ECONOMIC plight of the author a sufficient explanation of the sluggish condition of our writing? Reviewing Cyril Connolly's *Ideas and Places* recently [1953], V.S. Pritchett spoke of 'the thoroughly lost cause of the economic crisis in literature'. I find this interesting as coming from a man who has worked as hard as anyone to publicize the economic situation of authors, and I am sure Pritchett is right. Of course the crisis exists, but it is merely one factor among many making for our present sickness.

As Pritchett remarks – he was commenting on the *Horizon* questionnaire, 'The Cost of Living', reprinted in Connolly's book – 'Our claims have become so high or so low that they are meaningless.' What strikes one now as one reads the questionnaire is the muddle of thought and feeling revealed in it. In part, of course, when the author protests against his economic condition he is merely behaving like any other middle-class professional man whose standard of living has fallen. But when one looks at the answers to Connolly's questions one sees that the claims made by some of the contributors are conditioned by the social origins of those making them. They are a demand, in effect, that things shall be exactly as they were in Daddy's day. But at the same time there is a confused recognition that they cannot be. This indeed is the dilemma. We live and write at the fag-end of the romantic tradition. We are all, whether

80

we like it or not, imbued with the romantic conception of art. But that was based on the private income and the private patron. Now that both are gone it may be that a new conception of art is necessary.

REPAIRING THE DAMAGE

Rebecca West

The Authors' Contingency Fund was established in 1960 to provide short-term grants for writers in immediate financial need. Two years later we asked Dame Rebecca's help in alerting members of the Society to the new fund's plight, and her exemplary response appeared in the Summer issue.

CONRAD ONCE WROTE that it is the mark of an inexperienced man not to believe in luck, and, wise as he was, he never wrote wiser words. Certainly anybody whose experience has been gained in the literary field cannot believe that merit alone decides the success or failure of a writer. So true is this that the sensitive are aware of an acid aftertaste to the sweetness of any good fortune they may have. I know that one great man of letters and I myself share an unhappy feeling that any kindness the public may show us means little so long as a writer we think a genius goes quite unrecognized by that same public. And as for recognition, it can take a shaming form.

The largest sum I ever earned out of a single piece of work was from the sale of a story to a film corporation which in my youth I took down from the lips of another woman. Both she and I were paid large sums for the film rights. The film corporation used not a single incident nor a line of dialogue that was in my record, and it changed the title and the names of characters. What they had paid me for was a mystery, and I made it the more mysterious by insisting that my name was removed from the screen credits. A gift from a fairy godmother is less acceptable when she turns out to be the village idiot.

So we know it without any doubt: a writer who cannot maintain himself or herself may be a very good writer indeed. He may not have crossed the path of the village idiot at the right moment; he may have family unhappiness of a kind that eats up money and destroys peace; he may simply be out of fashion. . . .

An author may also fall into desperate trouble, ironically enough, because, though he is not a great writer, he has the kind of talent which educates writers and readers to produce and appreciate great books. His work may be too subtle in style and too scholarly in subject to appeal to any but the literary public. In which case he will find himself as he gets to middle age with a number of excellent but not very profitable publications behind him, and he will get small advances and have to live on all sorts of journalistic odd jobs. This kind of writer cannot save, and a bout of illness can do worse than empty his banking account, it can empty his pockets.

What is so dangerous to the writer labouring under such afflictions is that writing demands the full co-operation of the very thing in the mind which is distracted by private griefs and the fear of ruin. A writer who is in a position where he can make a case for receiving help from an organization because of his misfortunes is more unfortunate than even that proof demonstrates, for he is also in the position of a factory hand whose factory is burned down. He cannot help himself until the damage is repaired.

There are other tragedies, but these are the ones which we writers have been given power to understand and which are therefore a charge on our consciences. Happily we can acquit ourselves of this responsibility by contributing according to our capacity to the Authors' Contingency Fund, at 84 Drayton Gardens, SW10.

It is not necessary to give exact figures regarding the present deficit. There is never enough money in the fund to meet the calls that are made on it; and at the moment the till is nearly empty.

• • • •

One of the least impressive liberties is the liberty to starve. This particular liberty is freely accorded to authors. Otherwise the rewards they receive are pathetic, and even more pathetic is the absence of any real concern about their economic position and the immense difficulty of fomenting such a concern even in people whose love of literature is undoubted. . . . A civilized country ought not to leave its authors to find their own commercial levels of reward.

Lord Goodman, *The Times Literary Supplement,*
October 1970 (quoted in 'On the Side', Winter 1970)

AMERICAN EXPERIENCES

Although Bernard Shaw denied the validity of the term in the opening article of this anthology, the 'piracy' of British books by American publishers, because their country refused to recognize international copyright, was a long-rankling grievance of British authors in the nineteenth century. After the United States ignored the Berne Convention of 1886 Wilkie Collins, a member of the Society's Committee of Management, wrote a protesting article in the form of a letter 'addressed to an American friend'. Collins died (in 1889) before the article was published in May 1890, after being 're-covered by accident' from his papers. It remains by far the longest in the journal's history; from it we take the opening pages.

There is a great, a vast, increase in the United States of literary endeavour of all kinds . . . . If study and perseverance can make poets, novelists, and dramatists, then will the United States speedily lead the way. . . . It seems to me almost safe to prophesy an outburst before long of genius in the United States such as we ourselves have not seen since the time of Elizabeth. All the conditions are favourable – encouragement, honour, ambition, study, confidence, materials – everything is there waiting for natural aptitude or genius, and this will not be long before it shows itself in a full and flowing flood.

Walter Besant, February 1892

THOU SHALT NOT STEAL

Wilkie Collins

YOU WERE TAKING leave of me the other day, Colonel, when I received from the United States a copy of a pirated edition of one of my books. I threw it into the waste-paper basket with an expression of opinion which a little startled you. As we shook hands at parting, you said, 'When you are cool, my friend, I should like to be made acquainted with your sentiments on the copyright question.' I am cool now, and here are my sentiments.

I shall ask permission to begin by looking back to the early history of your own family. The fact is, that I wish to interest you personally in the otherwise unattractive subject on which I am about to write.

At the beginning of the seventeenth century, one of your ancestors, voyaging with the illustrious Hendrick Hudson, got leave of absence from the ship and took a walk on Manhattan Island, in the days before the Dutch settlement. He was possessed, as I have heard you say, of great ability in the mechanical arts. Among the articles of personal property which he had about him was a handsome watch, made by himself, and containing special improvements of his own invention.

The good man sat down to rest and look about him at a pleasant and pastoral spot – now occupied, it may be interesting to you to know, by a publishing house in the city of New York. Having thoroughly enjoyed the cool breeze and the bright view, he took out his watch to see how the time was passing. At the same moment, an Iroquois chief – whose name has, I regret to say, escaped my memory – passed that way, accompanied by a suitable train of followers. He observed the handsome watch; snatched it out of the stranger's hand; and, then and there, put it into the Indian substitute for a pocket – the name of which, after repeated efforts, I find myself unable to spell.

Your ancestor, a man of exemplary presence of mind, counted the number of the chief's followers; perceived that resistance on his single part would be a wilful casting away of his own valuable life; and wisely decided on trying the effect of calm remonstrance.

'Why do you take my watch away from me, sir?' he asked.

The Indian answered with dignity, 'Because I want it.'

'May I ask why you want it?'

The Indian checked off his reasons on his fingers. 'First, because I am not able to make such a watch as yours. Secondly, because your watch is an article likely to be sufficiently popular among the Indians to be worth. . . . Thirdly, because the popularity of the watch will enable me to sell it with considerable advantage to myself. Is my white brother satisfied?'

Your ancestor said that he was not satisfied. 'The thing you have taken from me,' he said, 'is the product of my own invention and my own handiwork. It is MY watch.'

The Indian touched his substitute for a pocket. 'Pardon me,' he replied, 'it is *mine.*'

Your ancestor began to lose his temper; he reiterated his assertion. 'I say my watch is my lawful property.'

The noble savage reasoned with him. 'Possibly your watch is protected in your country,' he said. 'It is not protected in mine.'

'And therefore you steal it?'

'And therefore I steal it.'

'On what moral grounds, sir, can you defend an act of theft?'

The chief smiled. 'I defend it on practical grounds. There is no watch-right treaty, sir, between my country and yours.'

'And on that account you are not ashamed to steal my watch?'

'On that account I am not ashamed to steal your watch. Good morning!'

The prototypes of modern persons have existed in past ages. The Indian chief was the first American publisher. Your ancestor was the parent of the whole European family of modern authors.

As time went on . . . the Republic of the United States started on its great career. With peace came the arts of peace. The American author rose benignly on the national horizon.

And what did the American Government do?

The American Government, having all other property duly protected, bethought itself of the claims of Literature; and, looking towards old Europe, saw that the work of a man's brains, produced in the form of a book, had been at last recognized as that man's property by the Law. Congress followed this civilized example, and recognized and protected the published work of an American citizen as that citizen's property.

Having thus provided for the literary interests of its own people within its own geographical limits, Congress definitely turned its back on all further copyright proceedings in the Old World. After a certain lapse of time, the three greatest nations on the Continent of Europe, France, Germany, and Italy, agreed with England that an act of justice to Literature still remained to be done. Treaties of international copyright were accordingly exchanged between these States. An author's right of property in his work was thus recognized in other countries than his own. It was legally forbidden to a foreign bookseller to republish his work for foreign circulation without his permission; for the plain and unanswerable reason that his work belonged, in the first place, to him and to no other person.

With this honourable example set before it by other Governments, what has the United States done? Nothing! To this day it refuses to the literary property of other people the protection which it gives to the literary property of its own people. To this day the President and Congress of America remain content to contemplate the habitual perpetration, by American citizens, of the art of theft.

THOU SHALT NOT
THROW STONES

Walter Besant

Below we publish an extract from an editorial by Walter Besant in 1891, shortly before the Chace Bill became law. That event was acclaimed as a victory over American isolationism by Besant, among others, although the limited copyright it offered was conditional on works being printed in the United States.

AMID THE GENERAL mingled chorus of denunciation, exasperation, disappointment, satire, and disgust, caused by the loss of the International Copyright Bill, there has hitherto been lacking – what it specially behoves *The Author* to supply – some recognition of the noble efforts made by the leading men, the men of culture, in the Eastern States. These men have never rested, and are still active, in advocating by every means in their power the passage of the Bill. They include all the authors of America, all the honourable publishers and a great number of editors. The opponents of the Bill are the ignorant Western farmers, who know nothing about literature, literary property, authors' rights, or anything else except their own local interests. The education of these men is a slow process; they take a great deal of time to grasp new ideas; the existence of authors is not suspected by them; the existence of authors' rights is absolutely unknown to them. But they are gradually being educated.

Let us consider our own case before we throw stones at the Americans. It is now five years since this society began

its endeavours to educate the British world into the perception of the fact that there is such a thing as literary property
and that it is a very real thing. We are not Western farmers.
Yet we have not learned to grasp this one central fact any
more than these honest members of Congress. Still the old
ideas cling; still those who talk of literary property as if it
was a real thing, like turnips, are regarded as madmen. Still
the leading articles talk of the dangers and uncertainties of
publishing. Still the old belief remains, that authors must
take whatever their employers choose to bring them; still
that old bogey, 'Risk', is trotted out to frighten us; still men
continue to talk about the 'generosity' of their publishers – as
if writers were beggars, humbly holding out their hands for
doles, instead of honest men demanding their just share in
the proceeds of the work of their hand and brain. These
ideas will slowly pass away. But meantime since they linger
in this country, and are every day traded upon for their own
purposes by interested persons, we cannot be surprised at an
equal ignorance among the narrow-minded and half-
educated people who form the greater part of Congress.

SOME NOTES ON A BILL

Rudyard Kipling

In the month before the Chace Bill became law The Author published the following poem by Rudyard Kipling, who was then on the Society's Committee of Management. We have left unedited the annotation of this literary curiosity, which does not appear in the author's collected verse. It was published in the United States in Harper's Weekly *a few days after its appearance in* The Author. *In 1920 it was published in a limited edition of 100 copies by the Pulaski Press at Little Rock.*

O peruse a simple Story – read a parable detached
From the vice of vending pullets ere the little beasts are
    hatched;
A weird, bi-lingual prophecy, with flying footnotes shored,
On the means of slipping sideways from the World's je-
    joggle-board.[1]

'Twas the Broncho[2] among Nations – a severely cultured
    race,
Though their mode of spelling centre proved them clearly
    off their base[3] –
Passed a Bill of three dimensions – two of which concerned
    the trade –
And one, but this was fiction, books the British Author
    made.

Softly sang the British Author, for a dream was in his brain
Of Landaus from Long Mere and of houses in Park Lane;
But ere he went to Tattersalls' or changed his modest
    dwelling
He explained, per Western Union, his objections to their
    spelling.

'Oh, my Largest Reading Public' thus the coded cable came,
'You drop one (hell) in "travelling" and – get there just the
    same:[4]
If to Webster and to Worcester, and your sauce at large I
    grovel,
It will vulgarize our fiction – taint the Holy British Novel.[5]

'Yet I'll vitiate the spelling of the Children of my friends,
If you pay me something extra for my labor.' (*Message ends.*)
And it filled that Author's system with severe electric shocks
When his Largest Reading Public cabled back: 'You're on
    the box.[6]

'The fact of being shouted for a dime along the cars
Does not fix you for a planet among Literary Stars;
Nor is it a safe assumption you can tetur continents
When our high-toned Mister H-rp-r[7] sews you up for fifty
    cents.

British parsons make us tired – British dukes, our daughters
    doubt 'em –
Cuss-words of the British Army, we can mosey on without
    'em;
Take a walk and get your hair cut[8] – sit on Mister M-d-e-'s
    shelves,
If we've *got* to pay for reading, guess we'll read about
    ourselves.'

So they read by free selection on a principle their own –
'Twas the most exhaustive weeding that an inkstained earth
   had known;
And the palpitating cable sizzled madly under sea,
'Honour without "u" I'll stomach; what is Honor without *me?*'

No, the fame the newsboys give you when they board the
   C.B.Q.
Does not predicate your kiting into honour without u.
If you cannot bang the big drum, you must twang the harp
   of Tara[9]
With McGinty[10] and O'Grady[11] and the man that struck
   O'Hara.[12]

It was good for Zenas Mather, Independence Psickafoos,
Adah Isaacs Menken, Shuswap, Janet, Thackeray, Van
   Dewze –
They stood pat as home-grown produce, with some seven
   thousand more
They were paid at full face-value – *they* came in on the
   ground floor.[13]

For they wove their country's fiction, triple-ply, of many
   shades,
From the big blue bergs at Sitka to the rotting Everglades;
And never since the Pilgrims furled the *Mayflower's* sea-
   worn sail,
Had the Bounder among Nations seen herself done out to
   scale.

It was woolly – wild and woolly – it was more than three feet
   wide,
For it ran from Maine to Oregon and out the other side.
With one nasal Hallelujah, like a giant Jew's hard drone.
The Bounder among Nations claimed a bookcase of her
   own.[14]

Now they're running ninety Shakespeares – all with variegated
  dictions,
They have put the growth of Miltons under interstate
  restrictions,
They brake the C.P. freight-cars with the Laureates of the
  West,
And a vigilance committee is sub-editing the rest.

They are writing of Proportion, and Reserve, and Racial
  Feeling,
Like an introspective sneak-thief who has just abandoned
  stealing,
And we can't attend to baby, and we can't lie down at night,
For those queer self-conscious schoolboys howl: 'Git up and
  see us write.'

But they're learning not to 'wiggle' when you photograph
  their manners;
They are guessing at a medium 'twixt 'you skunk!' and mad
  Hosannas;
And the men who know 'em fancy – if the measure they
  have made lasts –
That some day they'll be a Public – not a girl's school
  swapping Trade-lasts.[15]

Ends my lurid lucid legend, halts my parable divorced
From the blame of hunting Navajhoes before your scouts are
  horsed;
Oh, the Author's in the *purée*[16] and the dence is in the Bill,
But the Holy British Novel – yes – it's wholly British still.

[1] An elastic seat, found in the verandahs of Southern houses.

[2] An under bred animal with a swelled head, given to jumping nervously on inspection. *Anglice*: 'Bounder'.

[3] They are very like their babies, if you notice 'em they cry;
If you don't they steal your candy and their teachers call 'em 'Spry';
Their father's name was Washington – mis-statements made him wince –

But his sons declare on 'honor' – there's been no one like him since.

[4] Suppressed by Western Union as a *casus belli*. 'Your views of spelling "honour" match your notions on the same.' [Ed.]

[5] Now the Holy British Novel – from this verdict none shall warp us –
Is the Maiden's Magna Charta and the Matron's Habeas Corpus:
For when Maid and Wife have finished with the volume Father paid for –
You can read it to the Baby. This is what all books are made for.

[6] 'Come off the rocks' [Ed.]. *Anglice*: 'You labour under a misapprehension.'

[7] The leading sporting bookmaker of the United States. He does not bet on outsiders.

[8] Mutilated in transmission. Supposed to indicate esteem and personal interest.

[9] This instrument is distinguished for its enduring silences.

[10] Famous for his exploration of the depths of the Ocean.

[11] He was owed ten dollars – presumably on account of American royalties, for the money was never paid.

[12] The remains of this gentleman would not furnish a biography.

[13] *I.e.* There was no necessity in their case for abasement.

[14] They abandoned watered Herrick, and Elizabethan echoes,
They were not stuck on Browning like a horde of homeless geckoes,
'Twas a second Boston bust-up, but it cost us more than tea,
For the alphabet of authors they discarded – to a zee.

[15] Saidie tells Maimie that Hattie's new frock is pretty. Maimie repeats the compliment to Hattie, who tells Maimie that Saidie is 'just too sweet to live'. This is a trade-last. It is also called criticism.

[16] This is the position formerly occupied by the oyster.

ONE MAN'S AMERICA

Malcolm Bradbury

During this century the attitudes of many British writers towards the USA have been transformed: this is reflected in the following article by Malcolm Bradbury, published in Summer 1968 as the first in a series.

I SUPPOSE MOST writers have two points of reference between which they regularly oscillate – the provinces, which is the world of their upbringing, their families, their material often; and cosmopolis, which is the world where ideas and artistic experiments come from, the eternal Bohemian city. For many English writers in this century, the aesthetic forcing-house has been somewhere in Europe, and in particular Paris. For me – and, I suspect, for quite a number of post-war English writers – it has been the United States, and in particular the Bohemia of the American university campus.

As an undergraduate reading English in the 1950s, I found myself being steadily pulled toward American writing, particularly modern American writing (not that American literature was then being taught at my university, though it is now). When I started writing seriously, at around the same time, the writers who seemed best able to show me what to do and how to do it were, for me, mostly Americans. Less directly, I found, in a time when it seemed particularly hard to work out a way of living a satisfactorily independent literary life, America offered some useful and significant guidance. I went to the States as soon as I could, and I have kept on going there ever since.

If this pattern has any representativeness – and I think quite a number of English writers were independently taking the same sort of path – it reveals a significant shift in the balance of intellectual power. Until this century, most of the influence ran the other way; Europe was the cosmopolis and America the province. But in the post-war shifts of the intellectual and artistic scene, the States came out as a major influence – as a place where some of the most exciting literary advances were taking shape, where the most important ideas were being dealt in, where the possibilities (and tensions) open to the modern writer were being worked out. When I got to America, not as a resident expatriate but simply as a regular visitor, I found at once that it was easier to be the kind of writer I wanted to be. On the whole being a writer in England, certainly in the 1950s and probably still, seemed a lonely amateur occupation, unless one went for the highly professionalized branches like journalism or television writing. The climate in the States was much more explicitly favourable; writing was an encouraged activity, it was easy to meet other writers, and it was possible to get sponsored for being what one was.

One could explain all this cynically by saying that the prevailing economics were all behind it. The States weren't only the source of some of the liveliest and most relevant arts and ideas, but also of some of the most generous financial support for them: the great grant-giving nation, the country where the writer had a place on campus, a good range of fee-paying media, and good supplementary royalties. In particular, it was easy for the writer-teacher like myself to get to the States, by teaching or on fellowships, and once there to receive every encouragement for being a writer. The explicit regard for creativity there was of the greatest importance to me, since it was virtually not to be had in England at all. But even more the States suggested to me that there was a working relationship to be made between the two things that interested me most – writing and university teaching – and that the university campus could indeed be Bohemia, a place of intellectual and artistic ferment in which it was also possible to preserve a high degree of independence, economic and intellectual.

Of course it was true that campus-employed writers could and often did feel rather like the hermits employed by the eighteenth-century aristocracy as reminders of the life of unpropertied contemplation; but on the whole the alternative lives of literature, whether they were on Madison Avenue or Greenwich Village, seemed a good deal less independent. In an age when one of the biggest problems of the writer is defining a role and a social place, America helped and goes on helping.

But what was a good deal more important was the relevance of modern American experience, particularly literary experience, for our own English writing. For instance, it seems to me that the English novel has gone through a longish spell of aesthetic hang-up; in particular, it has found it singularly hard to mythicize – rather than simply to document – post-war British experience. One mark of all this is the virtual absence of aesthetic debate in the post-war English literary scene. We may indeed, as Al Alvarez has said, be in an age of No-Style; but the stylistics of No-Style have come in for a good deal more explicit discussion in the States than they have here. Our lack of aesthetic morale may go with loss of morale in other areas, but it has brought about a curiously unvivid period in English writing – with the possible exception of drama.

By contrast, American writing over the same period has gone through a remarkable phase of production and ferment, producing a body of really important writers (like Bellow, Mailer, Malamud, Powers and Roth in fiction) and a real aesthetic energy. It is this – much more, finally, than the advantageous economic arrangements that have also linked our two cultures closer together – that does most to explain the cultural shift I'm talking about, and the growing sense of respect many of us have acquired for American literary developments.

It's not easy to trace the consequences of this in modern English writing, since it penetrates into delicate matters like tonal assumption and the way we presume our audience to understand us. But I do think the United States is an inevitable influence on all of us, and in terms of literary evolution this has had good effects rather than bad – effects on our imaginations, our world-picture, the very tone of our writing.

The most obvious case for me was in my second novel, *Stepping Westward*, when I tried to make this relation between province and cosmopolis the theme of the book. The Anglo-American novel in the past has normally worked the other way, on the Jamesian model; set, as Henry James said, in 'the vaunted scene of Europe', it dealt with the encounter between the innocent American imagination and Europe's 'banquet of initiation'. The roles now seem to me very much reversed, imaginatively and humanly; and it was that reversal I set out to explore. Whatever the merits or otherwise of the book, the theme seemed to me, from my own point of view, inescapable. More and more, I think, the Anglo-American overview has had to enter into our literary understanding of our task, as for that matter in our total way of coping with experience.

MY FRIEND BARABBAS

During the past ninety-four years a great deal
of *The Author*'s space has been devoted to the
theory and the practice of author–publisher
relationships, good, bad and non-existent.
Although most of the contributions have come,
not surprisingly, from the writer's side, not all
of these put the publisher in the pillory. One
that did, entertainingly and instructively, was
by Bernard Shaw, reviewing *A Publisher's Confession* in July 1905. The book was published
anonymously in New York by Doubleday,
Page: the author was, in fact, its publisher,
Walter H. Page, who became an American
Ambassador to Britain. Later editions of the
book (e.g. that published by Heinemann in
1924) bore his name.

A publisher seeks out able people and urges them to write. He forms a relationship with his authors which recognizes that creative writing can be a painful effort. He helps to ensure that the author's words are in a form which both can proudly commit to permanence. He synthesizes, he organizes, he advises, he *edits*; editing is the touchstone of style and accuracy, a craft as old as the written word itself. . . . He links the creative act of writing with the equally creative act of reading.

Gordon Graham, then chief executive of Butterworth,
in a talk (quoted Summer 1980)

I object to publishers: the one service they have done me is to teach me to do without them. They combine commercial rascality with artistic touchiness and pettishness, without being either good business men or fine judges of literature. All that is necessary in the production of a book is an author and a bookseller, without any intermediate parasite.

Bernard Shaw, in a letter of 1895 from the first volume of Shaw's
Collected Letters, *edited by Dan H. Laurence (quoted Winter 1965)*

CONFESSIONS OF A BENEVOLENT AND HIGHMINDED SHARK

Bernard Shaw

THIS BOOK HAS the double charm of infinite comedy and obvious authenticity. Most confessions are spurious. Blameless wives of country clergymen have a mania for writing memoirs of improper females: city missionaries write autobiographies of convicted cracksmen: the penitent forms of the Salvation Army are crowded with amiable creatures confessing the imaginary brutalities they did not commit before they were converted. Confessions, in short, as Dickens succinctly put it, are 'all lies'. But this confession is genuine. The author is a real publisher from his bootsoles to his probably bald crown. There never was such a publishery publisher. The experienced author will read his book with many chuckles, and put it down without malice. The inexperienced author will learn from it exactly whom he has to face when he meets that most dangerous of all publishers, the thoroughly respectable publisher.

Need I add that the confession is not a confession at all? It contains only one admission: that publishers do not know how to advertise, and can do nothing more for a book than the book can do for itself. This, so far as it is true (and it is not wholly nor exactly true) is so obvious that there is no merit in confessing it. And the rest of the book is quite the reverse of a confession. It is an advertisement, an apology (in the classical sense), occasionally almost a dithyramb; and its tune throughout is the old tune, 'Won't you walk into my parlour?'

A few simple principles furnish our professing penitent with a solid moral basis. Of these the chief is that Nature ordains 10 per cent as the proper royalty for an author.[1] He makes no qualification as to the price of the book. It may be published at a shilling, or six shillings, or twelve shillings, or twenty-four. That does not matter. Nature does not fix the price of a book, though a dollar and a half is suggested as a desirable figure. She *does* fix the author's percentage – at 10. The penitent admits with shame that there are reckless publishers who offer more, and avaricious and short-sighted authors who are seduced by their offers. But bankruptcy awaits the former; and remorse and ruin are the doom of the latter. The book itself must needs be starved by cheap manufacture. The goose that lays the golden eggs (that is: the 10-per-cent publisher) is slain by that thriftless and insatiable grasper, the 20-per-cent author.

I shuddered as I read. For I too have a confession to make. I have not only exacted 20 per cent royalties; but I have actually forced the unfortunate publisher to adorn the dollar-and-a-half book with photogravures. It is quite true that the particular publisher whom I used thus barbarously actually did become bankrupt.[2] But he broke, not because he paid too high royalties, but because his profits were so large that he acquired the habits of a Monte Cristo, and the ambitions of an Alexander. Far be it from me to blame him or bear malice. I still believe in his star. Three or four more bankruptcies, and he will settle down and become a steady millionaire.

But the exaction of 20 per cent is not the blackest crime of which an author can be guilty. Our penitent is, in the main, kind to authors. I handsomely admit that authors are not angels – at least not all of them. Without going so far as to

---

[1] This view is strenuously combated by theatrical managers, to whom the Voice of Nature whispers 5 per cent as seemly and sufficient.

[2] Grant Richards, who went bankrupt that year. [Ed.]

say that some authors are rascals, I yet believe that authors have been known to practise on the vanity, the credulity, the literary ignorance, and the business flabbiness of publishers to get advances from them on books that remain unwritten to this day. Every season brings its budget of scamped, faked, and worthless books, feverishly pushed, to prove that those eminent and typical publishers, Alnaschar & Co., have again had their belly filled with the east wind by some duffer whose pretensions would not take in an ordinarily sharp bookstall boy. There are authors who make the poor publisher pay through the nose for nothing but their names in his list. For all these deceits and failures and oppressions our penitent has not a word of reproach. He forgives us everything, except DISLOYALTY. That is to him the one unpardonable and abominable sin. Loyalty, loyalty, loyalty, is what he asks before everything. To change your publisher is to become 'a stray dog' – his own words, I assure you. To bite the hand that fed you; to turn on the man who raised you from obscurity to publicity; to prefer another's 20 per cent to his 10: this is human nature at its worst. The pages of the confession almost blush as they record the shameful fact that there are viper authors who do this thing, and blackleg publishers who tempt them to do it.

Here is a powerful pen-picture of the polyecdotous authors. 'That man now has books on five publishers' lists. Not one of the publishers counts him as his particular client. In a sense his books are all neglected. One has never helped another. He has got no cumulative result of his work. He has become a sort of stray dog in the publishing world. He has cordial relations with no publisher; and his literary product has really declined. He scattered his influence; and he is paying the penalty.'

What an awful warning!

Yet, now that I come to think of it, I have done this very thing my very self. Dare I add that I would do it again tomorrow without the slightest compunction if I thought I could better myself that way. My publisher's consolation is that though I have no bowels, at least I do not pose as his benefactor, nor accuse him of disloyalty because he publishes books by other authors. Granted that an author with two or three publishers may seem (in America) as abandoned a creature as a woman with two or three husbands, what about a Solomonic publisher with half a hundred authors!

'Every *really* successful publisher', says our penitent (who is rather given to dark hints that the other publishers are not all they seem), 'could make more money by going into some other business. I think that there is not a man of them who could not greatly increase his income by giving the same energy and ability to the management of a bank, or of some sort of industrial enterprise.' May I point out that this is true not only of publishers but of all criminals, as many a judge has remarked before passing sentence. Whenever I meet a burglar, I always ask him why he runs such fearful risks, and performs such prodigies of skill and enterprise in opening other people's safes when he might turn publisher and be just as dishonest and ten times as rich for half the trouble. As to authors, I have yet met an author who was not convinced that if he put into business half the talent and industry he puts into literature, he could in ten years time buy up the Steel Trust that bought up Mr Carnegie.

The truth is, I suspect, that a publisher is an infatuated book fancier who cannot write, and an author is an infatuated book fancier who can. But the *Confession* does not urge this view, nor even mention it. According to it 'from one point of view the publisher is a manufacturer and a salesman. From another point of view he is the personal friend and sympathetic adviser of authors – a man who has a knowledge of literature and whose judgement is worth having.' Yes: I know that other point of view: the publisher's own point of view. I have had tons of his sympathetic advice; and I owe all my literary success to the fact that I have known my own business well enough never to take it.

Whenever a publisher gives me literary advice, I take an instant and hideous revenge on him. I give him business advice. I pose as an economist, a financier, and a man of affairs. I explain what I would do if I were a publisher; and I urge him to double his profits by adopting my methods. I do so as his personal friend and well-wisher, as his patron, his counsellor, his guardian, his second father. I strive to purify the atmosphere from every taint of a 'degrading commercialism' (that is how the *Confession* puts it), and to speak as man to man. And it always makes the stupid creature quite furious. Thus do men misunderstand one another. Thus will the amateur, to the end of the world, try to mix the paints of the professional.

I think I will give up the attempt to review this book. I cannot stand its moral pose. If the man would write like a human being I could treat him as a human being. But when he keeps intoning a moral diapason to his bland and fatherly harmonies about the eternal fitness of his 10 per cent on six shillings; his actuarial demonstrations that higher royalties must leave his children crying in vain to him for bread; his loudly virtuous denunciation of the outside publisher who publishes at the author's expense (compare this with his cautious avoidance of any mention of the commission system used by Ruskin, Spencer and all authors who can afford the advance of capital); his claim that all the losses caused by his endless errors of judgement are to be reckoned by authors as inevitable and legitimate expenses of his business; and his plea that his authors should take him for better for worse until death do them part: all this provokes me so that it is hard for me to refrain from describing him to himself bluntly in terms of his own moral affectations.

However, I will be magnanimous, and content myself with the harmless remark that the writer of the *Confession* is a very typical publisher. Publishers of a certain age always do go on exactly like that. The author's business is not to mind them, and to be infinitely patient with their literary vanity, their business imbecility, their seigneurial sentiments and tradesmanlike little grabbings and cheapenings, their immeasurable incompetence, their wounded recollections of Besant, their stupendously unreadable new book that is coming out the week after their timid refusal of the latest thing that does not reflect the chaos of second-hand impressions which they call their own minds; and the dislike of steady industry, the love of gambling, the furtive Bohemianism that induced them to choose their strange and questionable occupation.

As for me, all I ask on the royalty system at six shillings is a modest 20 per cent or so, a three years' trial, an agreement drafted by myself, and an unaffected bookseller. I don't want a compulsory partner for life. I don't want a patron. I don't want an amateur collaborator. I don't want a moralist. I don't want a Telemachus. I don't want a pompous humbug, nor a pious humbug, nor a literary humbug. I can dispense with a restatement of the expenses, disappointments, trials, and ingratitudes that pave the publisher's weary path to a destitute old age in a country house, with nothing to relieve its monotony but three horses, a Mercedes automobile and a flat in London. I have heard it so often! I don't expect absolute truth, being myself a professional manufacturer of fiction: indeed I should not recognize perfect truth if it were offered to me. I don't demand entire honesty, being only moderately honest myself. What I want is a businesslike gambler in books, who will give me the market odds when we bet on the success of my latest work.

No doubt this is a matter of individual taste. Some authors like the bland and bald-headed commercial Maecenas who loathes a degraded commercialism; tenders a helping hand to the young; and is happy if he can give an impulse to the march of humanity. I can only say that these benefactors do not seem to get on with me. They are too sensitive, too thin-skinned, too unpractical for me. The moment they discover that I am a capable man of business they retreat, chilled and disillusioned. Not long ago one of these affectionate friends of struggling authors, representing a first-class American firm, proposed to bind me to him for life, not by the ties of reciprocal esteem, but by legal contract. Naturally I said, 'Suppose you go mad! Suppose you take to drink! Suppose you make a mess of my business!' The wounded dignity and forgiving sweetness with which he retired, remarking that it would be better for the permanence of our agreeable relations if we let the matter drop, are among my most cherished recollections.

I hope I have not conveyed an unfavourable impression of what is – to an author at least – quite a readable, and not an unamiable little book. There are scraps of good sense and even of real as distinguished from merely intended candour in it, mixed up with some frightful nonsense about 'literary' books, our penitent being firmly persuaded, like most publishers, that a really literary book is one in which the word 'singularly' occurs in every third line, and in which 'I don't know where he went to,' is always written 'I know not whither he is gone.' But perhaps the best feature of the little book is the testimony it bears between the lines to the continued and urgent need for an Authors' Society.

In Winter 1932 Shaw recalled the repercussions of this review:

Instantly a distinguished author, by reflex action, rushed to repudiate me and defend the shark. And he was a Scot, too: no less a person than Andrew Lang, whom I had never injured, and whose interests I was defending. At the next dinner of the Society I took advantage of the speech-making to remonstrate with Andrew for betraying his profession for thirty pieces of silver (an understatement; but it pointed the moral). Andrew threatened to resign. As the sympathy was all with him, I was expected to withdraw or resign. As I did neither, Andrew resigned. I crowned my infamy by remarking, whilst the Society was supposed in literary circles to be staggering from this blow, 'And a good job too.'

THE SIN OF SILENCE

W.B. Maxwell

In October 1924 the bestselling novelist W.B. Maxwell, then Chairman of the Committee of Management, opened a series on authors and publishers. This is a shortened version of his article, which he introduced by declaring that he had 'found time to commit almost every indiscretion that is possible in the management of a literary career'.

I HAVE OFTEN thought that if anything could chill the ardour of an incipient author it would be a careful examination of this the official organ of our Society. The quarterly picture of the pains and penalties of authorship is so very black, so completely unrelieved by the least little flicker of light. One might think, if one did not know, that it is as dangerous to pass unarmed through Paternoster Row[1] (even in charge of a literary agent) as to linger solitary in the worst slums of Paris, Valparaiso, or Budapest; and that more wisely may one deposit one's notecase with a gang of confidence trick men in a sordid hotel lounge than put one's signature to a contract in a publisher's well-furnished parlour. When one reads the Secretary's cases, the solicitor's cases, the proceedings of the Committee, one feels that in comparison with this record of crime the Newgate Calendar is an innocent tale of trifles idyllically treated. . . .

[1] Until World War II, this was the site of many British publishers' offices and was a synonym for the trade. [Ed.]

Of course this aspect of gloom cannot be avoided. We are dealing with the dark side of the shield. In *The Author* as in *The Bulletin* (the excellent publication of the Authors' League of America) warnings to beginners, action taken on behalf of wronged members, with exposures of plagiarism, unpaid accounts, stolen rights, and so forth, necessarily occupy nearly all the space available. Not here can we dwell on the halcyon side of life. Not here must we sing our songs of joy, or echo the voice of an admiration tinged with envy telling us how glorious it is to need no other stock-in-trade than a bottle of ink and some blank paper, to have the world for one's workshop, and be able to label one's study door 'Anywhere'.

No, want of space forbids. But perhaps it might be possible to find some corner of every issue in which Mr Thring could keep a standing notice (very short) of reminders numbered one to five. As, for instance:

DON'T FORGET –

1 That there is nothing in the universe so fine in itself and so certain to make you happy as writing a good book, composing a splendid piece of music, or neatly constructing an actable play.
2 That *some* editors return manuscripts.
3 That the adjective 'bogus' does not apply to *all* theatrical managers.
4 That rates of remuneration are going up, not down.
5 That there are good publishers as well as bad ones.

I only throw it off as a suggestion. It would probably be a matter for the Annual General Meeting to decide.

There are good publishers and bad publishers – bad in the ascending scale of mediocrity, indifference, incompetence, crass stupidity, doubtful proceedings, sharp practices. On the other hand, the goodness of some publishers really amounts to a radiant steadfast altruism. It should be remembered too that a publisher may be good to one author and bad to another. . . . Publishers specialize just as much as authors. A man therefore should choose a publisher as carefully as he chooses a wife – and with the same pious hope of finding one to whom he can cleave till death do them part.

The advantages of sticking to the same publisher are obvious. You secure for yourself a business address that does not alter; the solid interest in your reputation held by the publisher goes on increasing; with many of your books in his hands he can afford to do more for each than if it were a single venture, he can also do more for them all together, in the way of cheap reprints, collected editions, and so on; he gives you regular and valuable advertisement in all his lists, because it is worth his while to do so; the whole bookselling trade know where to get your books, they buy them time after time from the same travellers, they, too, regard you with a steadily augmenting interest. Whereas if you dance about from publisher to publisher you lose much of all this. So far as the booksellers are concerned, you have at each change almost thrown yourself down into the position of a beginner. For booksellers hate change and are dangerously suspicious of it.

Moreover, it is idle to deny that even in this world of chaos and lost traditions the imprint of certain really good publishers has a prestige, if it does not quite bestow a cachet. The first question a reader asks of an author is, 'Who is your publisher?' and if one is able to reply 'So-and-So or Such-and-Such,' it has the same comforting sound as when one says one is a member of a still venerable and select club.

Unfortunately the imprudence of young writers is proverbial. Nearly all of us drift into authorship rather than deliberately taking it up as a trade. We deal with the first book we have written as though it may be the last book we shall ever write. Instead of wooing we succumb. Anybody may have us for the asking. And in a year or two, before we see the glow of dawning success, it often happens that we have fallen into several pairs of bad hands, have entangled and tied ourselves in such a web of foolish bonds that our whole future career, however successful it may be, is a long story of extrication.

Extrication! – That really sums up a very large part of this Society's work. In the case of young authors it is nearly always a compromised situation that we have to tackle. And in all sincerity I say that every person who has written a book and intends to publish it should become a member of the Society. The Society will tell him that, no matter how feeble and amateurish he may be feeling, he must treat his work in a serious businesslike manner. He must be as careful about his books as if they are going to live longer than *The Vicar of Wakefield, Paradise Lost*, or *Caesar's Commentaries*. It is a far-off chance; yet nevertheless he really must not be such an ass as to jeopardize it. . . .

Publishers commonly complain of the faithlessness of authors. The good publisher says authors have broken his confidence. He takes up an author; he admires him and believes in him; he publishes book after book at a loss; but he does not mind because he counts on ultimate success. Then just before the success comes the author leaves him; so that someone else reaps where he has sown. Publishers say also that if authors were not faithless there would be no necessity for future-mortgaging agreements, options, and the rest of the objectionable practices.

Authors leave publishers for many reasons, just as wives leave husbands. They leave because they think they are not being properly treated – that somebody else is being preferred to them – that in such an atmosphere they will never get an adequate chance of full self-expression. Sometimes they change their publishers merely from what may be described as night fears. They believe, quite baselessly, that the publisher has sold three large editions and accounted for only two meagre ones, that he did not 'remainder' that

115

masterpiece, but disposed of it at the ordinary price. They leave because, staring them in the face, there is the obvious fact that a new book to a publisher is a very small affair, while to them it is a very big one, since they are going to write only twenty more books and the publisher is going to publish ten thousand. They leave because their publisher is well satisfied with the modest measure of success they have obtained, while they are profoundly dissatisfied. They leave because of the sickness of hope deferred. They leave because other publishers are persistently beckoning and luring – not because, as the deserted publisher always thinks, a purse was rattled before their greedy eyes, but because a confident promise of improvement was given. They leave publishers in a large way of business because they are at last persuaded that their books get no proper show in an overcrowded list; they leave small firms because they have come to the conclusion that only the big capital, wide organization, and up-to-date management of a great concern can do them any good. But perhaps, above all else, they leave because of the publisher's besetting sin of *silence*.

The silence of publishers is awful. An author, whether young or old, wants to know what happens when his new book appears, but rarely if ever does the publisher tell him. On the day of publication not a word is said; on that day week, that day fortnight, the same ominous silence is preserved. Another mute week passes, and the author still doesn't know if one copy or a million copies have been sold – he knows nothing until, if he is lucky, he sees an advertisement of his work saying, 'Three editions exhausted in the same number of weeks. Fourth edition binding, fifth edition printing, sixth edition ordered.' But even then the publisher is still silent.

In this respect American publishers are better psychologists than their English confrères. They are quicker to put themselves in the other fellow's place. They understand all about the sickness of hope deferred. They send long cable messages, saying, 'Subscription sales disappointing, but your book just fine anyhow, and our boys here mean to push it for all they're worth. Will keep you informed.' That does one good – anyhow. They send one letters, press cuttings, advertisements. They tell one that their great-aunt likes it. And when finally they write to say that owing to unprecedented conditions, such a dam-burst of new literature this fall as has never before flooded the market, etc., etc – well, it may be the interment of a year's ambition, but at least it is a decent cheerful sort of burial. Moreover, American publishers make friends with their authors.

WANTED – A CIVILIZED
PARTNERSHIP

L.A.G. Strong

These extracts are taken from an article in Summer 1945 called 'The Author–Publisher Relationship, Past, Present, and Future'. Its author was especially well qualified to wrestle with the topic, as in addition to being a literary all-rounder – novelist, essayist, reviewer, playwright, biographer – he was a director of a publishing house, Methuen, for twenty years.

ALL THE EVIDENCE I have seen suggests that the entrance of the agent upon the literary scene is one of the best things that have ever happened to the trade of authorship, and therefore, to the publishing trade. For the interests of these two trades are one and the same interest, and the sooner they realize it the better. To them I would add the book-sellers. The book trade is an indivisible unit. Nothing short of the fullest and friendliest collaboration between its indispensable parts can be to the best interest of any one of them. But booksellers are out of my text.

Until a comparatively short while ago, it would have been fair to say that, on the whole, publisher and author saw themselves less as partners than as potential opponents. In the last century – to judge by the memories of many authors – the publisher had the better of the struggle. Only the few very successful authors could oblige him to vary his terms. As the capitalist who financed the deal, the publisher was in a commanding position. Even in this century, a glance into the records of some of the more old-fashioned firms shows (to put it in modest terms) a number of extraordinarily one-sided bargains in which the author was not on the winning side. My own experience does not go back very far, but I have been offered contracts of which I was obliged to redraft every clause which I did not cut out altogether, and a few contracts with which I would have no truck at all. I have had the pleasure, too, of preventing beginners from signing documents which would barely have left them the mattress on their bed. What is more, some of the firms offering these documents for signature bore well-known names, and/or were connected with some form of religious organization.

A great deal of the hokey-pokey which has marred the relationship in the past has been possible only because neither side was a united body. There have been publishers willing to take advantage of other publishers, and authors ready to take advantage of other authors. The publisher who poaches, who tempts an author away from a colleague with the bribe of a big advance, encourages that author in an enterprise which worsens the entire author–publisher relationship. The author who undercuts a colleague, who in ignorance, need, or sheer selfishness accepts inequitable terms which other authors have refused, strengthens the hand of the publisher unscrupulous enough to offer those terms, and therefore of the unscrupulous publisher everywhere.

Of the two classes, I regret to confess that, in my experience, authors show less sense of solidarity than publishers, and less regard for their contractual obligations. Although I am on the board of a publishing house, and had experience before that in another, I remain, always and obdurately, an author. My allegiance has never faltered. But, insomuch as it is easier for an author to wriggle out of a contract than for a publisher, in point of fact authors do so wriggle more than do publishers. . . for the simple reason that it can never pay any publisher to keep hold of a

119

dissatisfied author. The best thing is to let him go, and quickly. Therefore, in their own interest, publishers allow the author (and his agent) rather more latitude in interpreting the clauses of a contract than author or agent will allow them.

No one can be long in contact with the officers of the Society of Authors, as it has been my good fortune to be for some years, without seeing how wastefully and pointlessly things can go wrong when either publisher or author tries to steal a march on the other. Unilateral action is bound to be resented, and probably misunderstood, by the side which has not been consulted. Publishers need to be especially considerate in this respect. It is far easier for them to combine than it is for authors. For one thing, there aren't nearly so many of them.

If it is agreed that a friendly partnership between publisher and author is the ideal – and I do not see how this can be disputed, since each is indispensable to the other – the next thing is to consider practical measures for enabling and maintaining such a relationship. Here I expect I am on dangerous ground, since everyone will have his own ideas. For what they are worth, mine are on the lines that follow: and they have this one qualification at any rate, that they are based upon experience on both sides of the fence.

First of all, I would like to see a committee composed of elected representatives of authors and publishers, in equal numbers, with powers to discuss and decide all questions which concern both. Such a committee would make it impossible for one body to make a decision affecting those questions without the agreement of the other.

Second, we badly need some measure which will bring contracts between author and publisher into line. Any standardized form of contract is, of course, impossible. Authors' terms vary with their status, and some publishers cannot afford the advances given by others. But it is more than time that there was agreement as to the rights a publisher may fairly claim, and those which belong to the author. I have seen contracts offered to beginners which gave the publisher all subsidiary rights. I have seen a contract from a publisher of high standing which claimed 50 per cent of the film rights. (The film rights were sold, and the publisher, feeling twinges of conscience, reluctantly returned 25 per cent.) This question of subsidiary rights has never been thrashed out; at least, if it has, the publishers have kept the secret to themselves. In practice, each publisher does what he thinks fit about it. Many claim large percentages of these rights in their printed forms of agreement, and excuse themselves by saying that it is open to the author to negotiate. This is all right, if he knows enough about it, or has an agent. Hundreds of authors, especially beginners, have not these advantages, and make their publishers handsome and unintended presents.

Obviously, the Society of Authors can be invaluable in helping to establish points of this kind: but – dare I hint it? – there is a danger that even it (I mean we) may tend to see ourselves as skilled bargainers getting an advantage over 'the other side'. It is difficult, with the best will in the world, to avoid this attitude sometimes: to avoid the suggestion that one side or the other has been trying something on, and has got the worst of the subsequent exchanges. That must go. Impossible? I don't believe it. Every author's publisher should be his or her good friend. Every publisher's authors should be his good friends. It makes life simpler. It pays. It is more civilized. That much of the world will be easier, happier, better run. That garden will be better cultivated. And, in the years ahead, the more well cultivated gardens there are, the better our chances. . . .

A STUDY IN EXTREMES

Michael Holroyd

The biographer of Lytton Strachey, Hugh Kingsmill and (in due course) Bernard Shaw contributed this piece, under the main title of 'Authors and their Publishers', to The Author *in Spring 1969.*

BARABBAS IS THE exceptional, not the typical publisher. But the difficulty of the author–publisher relationship must always be that their interests are sometimes identical, sometimes directly opposed. As every publisher knows, the maladies most incident to authors are egocentricity and paranoia. Blinkered by these, the author cannot understand why his publisher should be so skilful before signature of the contract, so inept after publication day. The combativeness of some authors, it seems, puts the publisher on his mettle; while the vast dough of the public reduces him to slumber.

Traditionally, as every author knows, incompetence is the special talent of publishing. Once, it was an occupation for gentlemen, ex-debutante secretaries and an office cat, and the incompetence was leisurely, decorative. Now it has been invaded by American school of business methods, by computers that give out rows of Xs instead of the elusive sales figures, by the interests of television, newspapers, even bus companies. The resulting chaos is energetic, formidable, but usually not unfriendly. I have been in one publisher's office where a director was dictating a letter on the most modern machine to a French colleague in Paris, while that colleague sat next door discussing with a fellow director the very matter about which he was being simultaneously consulted only a few feet away. Yet not a smile breaks, not an eyebrow lifts, not a forehead creases at incidents such as this – they are everyday affairs.

One of the fascinations in writing the lives of authors is to explore the relationships they had with their publishers – and compare them to one's own. Of the two writers whose biographies I have written, Hugh Kingsmill and Lytton Strachey, one was uncommercial, the other, after much struggling, highly successful. Their experience of publishers differed widely.

After his first book, *Landmarks in French Literature*, which was brought out as one of a series by Williams and Norgate, Strachey stayed for the rest of his career with a single publisher. Kingsmill stayed with no one, for long. There were few London publishers from whom he did not extract, at one time or another, an advance, very often for one of his anthologies, which he would foist on whoever was bringing out his most recent book. This was his standard way of dealing with the option clause in his contract. Having the advantage of possessing no business brain, he was inclined to treat any money given to him in advance as a quite separate matter from the royalties themselves – a sort of pledge of faith that had no connection with the eventual sales, and that it was quite unethical to deduct later on. After all, he once pointed out, they were very tiny amounts – more of retreats, really, than advances.

In their financial aspect, publishers were *in loco parentis* for Kingsmill – which may explain why, in spite of all his infuriating habits, they continued to find him endearing. With rugged optimism, he expected to get from them what his father, Sir Henry Lunn, was unwilling or unable to hand over himself. And, from his point of view, he managed them very ably. From Jonathan Cape, Robert Hale and Macdonald he certainly received advances without getting round to supplying any books, and from Methuen he received a number of such sums. 'Annually when our auditors checked our books', wrote Alan White of Methuen, 'I was asked by my boss to account for these sums. Piqued by his tone, I said tartly that works of the imagination could not be written with mechanical regularity. He stared a full minute at his papers, and then remarked, without the trace of a smile (though he was not without humour on subjects unconnected with business): "Works of the imagination is right."' But when at last a book was produced, it was written so well, and sold so badly, that the publisher and Kingsmill himself were reduced to despair – at which moment another anthology was born. He was, in the words of Rupert Hart-Davis, 'the publisher's nightmare'.

It was Rupert Hart-Davis who, while he was working at Cape, commissioned Kingsmill to write his autobiography. The late Jonathan Cape told me, when I was writing my biography, that in his opinion Kingsmill was neither a very pleasant personality nor a writer of any great talent, but on further questioning admitted never having known him or read his books. Rather naïvely perhaps I pressed him to explain his views, at which he pointed out that Kingsmill had never completed his autobiography, for which he had nevertheless received money. With a flourish he then handed me the original contract with the air of a magistrate producing a criminal document. Choosing to overlook the several years that had elapsed between the date on the contract and Kingsmill's final illness and death, I exclaimed: 'But he died!' Mr Cape looked at me coldly for what seemed a very long time. 'And whose fault was that?' he demanded.

It was his unending money difficulties that drove Kingsmill to use his publishers so desperately; and it was his irresponsible attitude that persuaded publishers not to commission from him those very books that he would have written best. The sort of author who replied to their letters on the backs of writs was not, they reasoned, quite the proper person to entrust with a major literary undertaking. They were wrong, though their attitude is understandable.

Strachey was cushioned against the awful poverty Kingsmill experienced and, largely for that reason, inspired his publishers with greater confidence. He was recommended by his friend Clive Bell to send the typescript of *Eminent Victorians* to Chatto & Windus. 'And how very strange to be published by Chatto & Windus!' he had himself written to Bell four years beforehand, just after Bell's little book *Art* had been published. 'I thought they did nothing but bring out superannuated editions of Swinburne variegated with the Children's Theological Library and the Posthumous Essays of Lord de Tabley.'

Nevertheless it was to Chatto & Windus that *Eminent Victorians* was sent. Its two readers, Geoffrey Whitworth and Frank Swinnerton, were 'as excited before publication as the world was after it'. But when it was published, on 9 May 1918, almost the only people from whom Strachey heard nothing were the publishers themselves who, in that quaint way publishers have, assumed that the author's interest in his work had ceased on publication day. They had brought it out at the price of 10s 6d allowing Strachey 15 per cent of this on the first 1,000 copies sold, and 20 per cent thereafter – this for what, to all intents and purposes, was a first book!

They had also undertaken to pay him a £50 advance on the day of publication, but the weeks went by and nothing happened. 'It's rather awkward,' Strachey nervously admitted to Clive Bell. 'Ought I to write to Geoffrey Whitworth? Perhaps if I'm patient it'll all come right – but perhaps not.' Soon afterwards a letter from Geoffrey Whitworth did turn up. It made no mention of the advance, but it contained a phrase that deserves to become a publisher's classic. *Eminent Victorians*, he explained almost with regret, was selling so well that 'we are being *forced* to *think about* a reprint'. Strachey commiserated, but also brought up the matter of the non-existent advance, and by return of post received a cheque with apologies.

After this false start, the relationship between Strachey and Chatto & Windus grew to be extraordinarily cordial. They are always seeking out ways and means to pay him extra money (without any prompting from Strachey), always improving the mouth-watering clauses in his contracts and subsequently breaking them for his increased benefit. They press him not to hurry with his next book; they offer to grapple with the tax authorities on his behalf; they send him innumerable dust jackets and alternative bindings from which he is asked to select his favourite; then out of the blue they write to congratulate him, in general terms, on nothing in particular, and urge him, for his own protection, to submit all negotiations to the Society of Authors. They even arrange for him to witness the printing of his books, though the moment he appeared all the machinery broke down and came to a halt, much to their confusion – and probably to Strachey's relief.

And Strachey, too, is the last word in courtesy. He invariably makes pressing enquiries after the health of the partners (even the retired ones), apologizes for the slightest delay and for the legitimate correction to proof copies, recommends a friend of his to join the firm, will not listen to offers from other publishers. Perhaps bestselling authors still enjoy relationships such as this. But for the rest of us it is something to savour in all its charm, and to marvel at long and deeply.

• • • •

We have read your manuscript with boundless delight. If we were to publish your paper, it would be impossible for us to publish any work of a lower standard. And as it is unthinkable that in the next thousand years we shall see its equal, we are, to our regret, compelled to return your divine composition, and to beg you a thousand times to overlook our short sight and timidity.

From the *Financial Times*, whose columnist, 'Observer', declared this to be a genuine rejection slip from a Chinese economic journal (quoted Winter 1980)

THE SEARCH FOR PATRONS

Long before the Arts Council's Literature Department was set up with a token budget in the mid-1960s, the need for literary patronage (in the broadest, non-pejorative sense) had become apparent to many writers who viewed the possibility of state aid as both remote and/or dangerous. Our first extracts date from October 1902, when Herbert Trench, among other enthusiasts, was urging the establishment of an Academy of Letters, and H.G. Wells was on the other side. Sir Osbert Sitwell's plea comes from a symposium on 'The State and the Arts' in Spring 1944, to which Rose Macaulay contributed. Four years later in Spring 1948 this was followed by Sir Herbert Read's 'First Aid for Authors'. A year later *The Author* opened its Spring issue with an editorial on 'Young Talent', from which we publish an extract.

It is beginning to be commonly accepted that creative writing must be a by-product of life, a thing to be intermittently undertaken in odd moments of tired leisure in a working week devoted to teaching, or to journalism, or a job in the BBC, or in a publishing firm. I hope I shall not be accused of a derogatory view of these careers and activities if I say that, in my opinion, they are ultimately injurious, perhaps even fatal, to the poet, the novelist, the dramatist.

Rosamond Lehmann, in a letter to the editor,
Spring 1949

Herbert Trench

WE MUST NOT look for help from the 'upper classes'. The French courtiers of the seventeenth-century salons, the eighteenth-century groups of English country gentlemen round Pope and Addison, round Johnson and Burke, were recruited from educated aristocracies. It was these gentlemen who formed noble libraries, and paid for splendid editions. They had gone on the 'grand tour' to France, Italy, and Greece, to the older and wiser civilizations, and so had improved a naturally good eye for the tasteful and the humane. But the modern grand tour is to the United States for a rich wife. Or our young aristocrat, if more wholesomely disposed, returns with the imperfect tastes of frontier peoples. Our young barbarian becomes accomplished in Rhodesia or the Klondike. He returns, perhaps, no worse a man than were the sons of Halifax, Temple, Fox, Walpole or Chesterfield. But as a judge of letters he is probably less complete. In our quandary no help is to be expected of him. No help, either, from our mob-deity the millionaire, who may found libraries till every Sheffield has its British Museum, yet cannot provide a living for literature. No! The writers of England, if they are to restore the dignity of their craft, must do it themselves. Their task, owing to the vast augmentation of the reading populace, and the all-pervasiveness of vulgar wealth, is harder far than it was for any French king or English aristocracy. But, on the other hand, is not that task tenfold better worth the doing? Its result may be the gradual

129

ennoblement, not of a clique in a capital, but of an entire nation. . . .

'Treasure words,' said Gogol; 'they are the noblest gift of God.' And the object I have in writing these lines is boldly to ask those who have the honour of English letters at heart to form themselves into a 'Guild of Literature', as did the craftsmen painters of Flanders and Italy – a guild open to any fairly accredited writer to join. From this guild should be elected, chiefly (I think) by writers themselves, a number of leaders – Masters of the Craft – to protect it, to represent it, and do it honour.

Such a public association of the distinguished and en-lightened would act, as Lucas Malet says, as an immense encouragement to the rank and file of writers, especially those of the younger generation. It would stimulate to steady work – concentrate attention on noble ambition and pure reward. It would help year-long labour like 'that slow and scientific' labour of Titian. It would secure for living writers praise and recognition far earlier than now is possible.

H.G. Wells

I DON'T THINK AN Academy of Letters can possibly be invented to do what those who advocate the establishment of one desire. It would be admirable if we *could* have a body to 'hallmark'. . . what is really of fine quality so soon as it appears, but the nearest approach we can ever get to such a body is a large well-educated reading public, keenly interested in criticism; and even then there will be winds and currents of favour.

The chief objection to Mr Trench that occurs to me is the fact that a man may be a quite splendid figure in contemporary literature, and yet spend remarkably little time in the research after contemporary merit, much less contemporary promise. . . . There are men to whom no one would deny the crowns and glories of literature, but it is another matter to ask them to control its destinies. Mr Trench, like most Academy projectors, overlooks the fact that a new addition to literature is almost invariably a breach of the established boundaries, a variation of style, matter, treatment, a revelation of new aspects and new thoughts. I do not see that it is reasonable to expect the Old Men, resting gloriously amidst their accomplished work, to bother about the New Men, or to assimilate the new views. They are far more likely to fill their gaps with the Scholarly Gentleman, the Able Imitator – quite apart from wire-pulling and intrigue and the natural desire of those who have arrived and are accepted to lead a pleasant life.

Far more efficient to the end Mr Trench desires would be an Academy of lively and contemporary critics – Messrs Gosse, Edward Garnett, Waugh, Bennett, William Archer, Street, Chesterton, for example – but even then. . . . Probably they would never be sufficiently agreed to elect anybody. And before ever you come to the question of replacement you have to consider that you will never get a really literary Academy as things are at present. You will get a few indisputable literary figures, the conscience members one might call them, and the rest will be men who are really only well-bred influential amateurs, men no one would dream of putting into an Academy if they had done just exactly what they have done now from the starting point of a lower-class home. There are Mr Balfour, for example, and Lord Rosebery. You will never be able to float an Academy without this element unless you have that educated public we need – and then your Academy, I submit, will be totally unnecessary.

The Good Outsider, that Intrusive Bounder, who is the living soul of literature, will be left outside anything Mr Trench and his fellow workers can possibly invent, and the Uninspired Respectability will be in – from the very beginning. It is inherent in the nature of Academies and unavoidable. You don't get 'hallmarked' till you are dead and a little obsolete. This is sad for the innumerable authors now palpitatingly conscious of superlative merit, but it is one of the things you have to make your peace with in the literary life.

Sir Osbert Sitwell

In his heart, the artist knows that the world, hostile to him since his birth, is never more inimical than when it pretends to be friendly. He remembers how the man in the condemned cell is called on the morning of his execution, how he is asked to choose his breakfast. He realizes what the state as patron involves: glittering prizes would soon bring his genius level with that of the contemporary politician. It means pandering to the aesthetic sense of the town council, to that of every oaf, who says 'I know what I like'; it means hearing archbishops delivering their views about the excellence of the limerick and the tedium of Milton or the moral lapses of taste of Thomas Hardy. It means Lord Wavell's Anthology. It means, perhaps, a livelihood in this existence, but no survival after it. Above all, it means endless exhibitions of war pictures, and an endless output of war books. For a world in which the state is patron is a world in which no other patrons exist, a world in which the state is omnipotent. And such a state, since it thrives on war, always heads for it – either consciously, by being so provocative as to plunge the country into it, or unconsciously by being so unprepared as to achieve the same result.

As for a Minister of Fine Arts, he would achieve for living art what the National Trust and the Office Works accomplish for old buildings. The studio of the artist would be garnished and sterilized and be made empty – but alas the Seven Devils of Art would not enter in. What the artist wants from the state is not employment; but simply money! What we want from those who govern the state is not art patronage, but less muddle. For public money is merely private money put together; and the artist will always find patrons if the money is there.

Rose Macaulay

HERRICK, ADDRESSING Mr Endymion Porter, said, 'Let there be Patrons, Patrons like to thee, Brave Porter!' and goes on to tell him that he supplies 'not only subject-matter for our wit, but likewise oil of maintenance for it'. The second provision is, of course, the one we want; it does not do at all when patrons, either state or otherwise, begin thinking they will supply the subject-matter for our wit; that way lies the danger of state art. Yet how to avoid the danger altogether, if oil of maintenance is to be handed out to some artists and not to others? There must be selection, and selection implies weighing of deserts; unless indeed the maintenance is to go entirely on grounds of need, to help all frail plants to grow, while those who can manage without it push their own way up as now. If so, there will be no censorship as to quality; the tough, low dandelion growth will go on disseminating itself as freely, as ineradicably, as now. But not all the needy artists can or should be helped; there must necessarily be a choice on merit. And who would make it?

Herbert Read

No MEANS HAS yet been devised of rendering first aid to literature, which is certainly badly in need of it, and has no prospect of getting it from any other source [but the state]. . . .

Quite naturally, it is feared that the handing out of monetary grants to individual authors by a public corporation would be open to all kinds of abuse. There is no clear escape from this dilemma, but of one thing I feel sure: the solution is to be found only by authors acting in their corporate capacity or, more bluntly stated, through the Society of Authors. Originally conceived as a protective association, our function in future will have to be more positive. In a form of economy which tends more and more to become corporative, based on functional organization, authors must be prepared to act as a body. . . .

The central problem is the practical support of those types of literature which are no longer viable in an economy of mass production. We must find some method, extensive in scope, harmless in application, which will secure the publication of, and adequate reward for, those categories of literature which I have specified [poetry; literary criticism and scholarship; and the essay].

The universities might do more for scholarship. I do not see why every university in the country should not have its press, subsidized from its normal funds. But not all scholarship is university scholarship, and though university presses might be encouraged to publish works of extra-mural scholar-ship, there should be some independent medium of publi-cation. This might well be the same as that established for poetry and *belles-lettres*.

I must now tread warily. I belong to that anomalous group of author-publishers, far more numerous than is usually realized, which is a characteristic feature of this transitional age. My loyalties are divided, but looking to the future, I do not think I compromise my trade if I suggest that it should be prepared to hand over to some disinterested body that part of its business which it no longer finds profitable, and merely retains for reasons of prestige or charity. The balance sheets of our great publishing houses would not be materially affected if they ceased from tomorrow the publication of poetry and literary criticism, and most publishers would rejoice to be relieved of the unprofitable burden of vain solicitations which such publication encourages.

Admittedly, in a few rare cases, there comes a stage (after many years of waiting in the outer court) when the publishing of poetry or criticism becomes commercially profitable. It is not safe to assume, however, that these cases preserve either the continuity of a literary tradition or guarantee its highest achievements. Blake, Coleridge, Keats, Shelley, and Landor were never, in their lifetime, regarded as 'profitable invest-ments'. The future of English poetry would not have been preserved by an exception like Byron or Tennyson. And today there are no Byrons or Tennysons.

I suggest, therefore, that no harm would be done to the trade, and much good might be done for the art of literature, if some chartered corporation, similar to the Arts Council or even sheltering under its wing, were to be established for poetry and *belles-lettres*. It would have its grant from the Treasury, just as the Arts Council has its grant; and there is no reason to suppose that it could not be administered as fairly and as fruitfully as is the Arts Council itself. The Society of Authors and the Publishers Association would, of course, have their representatives on the Literature Panel of the Arts Council. Its publications would not be sold at 'trade prices'; they would be 'given away' to literary and educational institutions. Individual copies might be sold to the public at nominal prices, comparable to the prices charged for catalogues of the Arts Council's exhibitions.

In the end, it is merely equal treatment we ask for our literary arts; for why should the other arts have a monopoly of public patronage?

I call this a 'first aid' measure, because I am not for a moment assuming that the life and nourishment of any art is dependent on the patronage it receives. The process is much more mysterious than that, and no patronage can confer greatness on an art whose roots are withering in an impoverished soil. First aid is like rain in a dry season; but fertility depends on organic processes over which, I suspect, we have very little power of conscious control.

Editorial

AUTHORSHIP IS NOW so far from being even relatively lucrative that it is hardly self-supporting. The costs of producing books have almost put an end to 'prestige' publishing. Poetry is nearly unpublishable. Even the novel, the interpreter of contemporary life, is . . . coming to be regarded as primarily 'the book of the film'. Writing for the theatre is in not much better case. There is state aid for British acting and presentation, but for the would-be dramatist the theatre is Heartbreak House: he cannot live through the preliminaries of getting a play produced. And perhaps the most damaging thing of all is that experimental writing, the mine from which a generation of later writers may draw dynamic influences (Joyce's *Finnegans Wake*, for example), is in danger of being abandoned.

In these strange new rigours very few writers find that they can earn a living by writing books. Established writers, from whom it would be normal to expect not only solid contributions but new and vital impulses as their experience and perceptions deepened, have had to turn to other ways of supporting themselves and their families: to reviewing, editing; writing script, copy, articles; to the Civil Service, the British Council, the BBC, schools, publishers' offices. It is all to the advantage of those callings and bodies, but very much to the detriment of our national literature. Creative energy is expended in routine and writing ephemeral matter. Creative writing is a luxury which needs a settled income. A young writer can no longer rent a room or an unused cottage for a few shillings a week and live, for a valuable year or two, on next to nothing but the joys and hardships of creation. And he has no achievement to trade for a job.

Out of all this there has come the imperative question: Is the essentially individual life of the creative artist to find its true expression in the new social organization and economy, or is literature to fall into a settled mediocrity from which the community will draw neither the inspiration nor the guidance which is the real value of all free art?

One answer to that question is found in the view that good writing, like good men, cannot be kept down in any circumstances; that it is all the better for its creator's struggles and difficulties – indeed, that it needs and thrives on such things; that if there is no great literature at a given time it is because there are no writers of the quality that produces it. As far as it goes it is certainly a true answer; but it may not go far enough to be a complete one. It leaves out of account the nature of patronage and its fundamental relation to literature and the arts. That is a subject that needs examining fully. All that can be said about it in these limits is that literature has flourished without direct patronage only when the cost of living was low during the prosperous period of capitalist industry which the two wars closed. Patronage may mean different things at different times. In our time it means leisure, which has never been so hard to come by. Without it there may be art in the Crocean sense but there are no works of art, no literature.

The other answer proposes a revival of patronage; and in the new economy the state is the only capitalist body which could effectively patronize the arts. It is already doing so, indirectly, through the Arts Council. But to suggest that it should become a direct patron of literature is to bring at once to mind that in certain countries authorship has shrunk to the utilitarian dimensions of a political instrument. Instead of receiving the enlightened fathering of true patronage it is subject to rigid control; consequently it is insulated from the freely formative air of literature. . . .

The Society of Authors is closely considering a plan to which its President [John Masefield) drew attention in a letter to *The Times* last October. It is proposed that the Treasury should make an annual grant, for an experimental period of three years, of a sum of money to be administered by a committee of writers of the highest integrity. The committee's function would be to make awards purely on literary merit, but on the widest possible terms according to the needs and circumstances of each case, which the committee's collective experience would enable it to assess.

The proposal outlined in the Poet Laureate's letter is aimed at aerating and enlightening the circumstances of genius. It has provoked wide discussion and a number of suggested modifications: that, for instance, the state could help more effectively by removing the crippling anomalies in the taxing of authors' earnings, by lifting restrictions on travel, by looking for a means of easing the costs and delays of publishing. What seems to be emerging from the debate so far is that there is an urgent need to take stock of the state of our literature and to consider ways of enriching it; that financial help, either from the State or from a fund which the establishment of a 'domaine public payant' would provide, could be effectively applied in an agreed direction if its administration were free of political and departmental control. . . . Authorship has fallen on such evil times that a national plan to make it a field of opportunity again may be the only way of bringing life back into our literature.

PUBLIC RELATIONS

In January 1925 the top-selling novelist W.B. Maxwell, then Chairman of the Society's Committee of Management, contributed a provocative piece on 'Authors and their Public', abridged below. This was challenged by John Galsworthy in the April issue of *The Author* and by Hugh Walpole in a letter published in July. As postscripts to the debate we include an excerpt from a letter to *The Author* from Nevil Shute, written in 1951, and an expedient proposed by Bernard Shaw in July 1903.

I never *courted* the public – and never will yield to it. As long as I can find a *single* reader I will publish my Mind (while it lasts) and write whilst I feel the impetus. As to profit, that is another matter – if none is to be attained – it must be dispensed with. Profit or loss – they shall never subdue me while I keep my senses.

Lord Byron, in a letter of 1821, from In the Wind's Eye, *the ninth volume of Leslie Marchand's edition of his letters and journals (quoted Autumn 1979)*

The Public and the reviewers have always given way, and always give way, to the idiosyncrasies of an author who is strong enough to make them. The history of literature is nothing but the performance by authors of feats which the best experience had declared could not be performed.

Arnold Bennett in a letter of 1904 to J.B. Pinker, from Letters of Arnold Bennett, *vol. 1, Oxford University Press, 1966 (quoted Winter 1966)*

W.B. Maxwell

I HAVE NEVER been able to understand the mental attitude of certain writers who say, and apparently quite sincerely, that they write to please themselves and do not in the least care how many or how few readers they have. Or in other words, that pleasing themselves they do not mind if they fail to please anybody else. The desire for the greatest possible number of readers seems to me not only justifiable, but a proper ambition for every writer to entertain. A readerless author is in an unenviable position from all points of view. He is like a messenger on an errand that has no destination, like a statesman unfolding his policy to an empty Albert Hall, like a man making love on the telephone after the object of his affection has hung up the receiver and switched off at her end of the wire.

Moreover with regard to *pleasing*, if we take the world in its widest sense, there is, as R.L. Stevenson pointed out, a tacit obligation on the part of the author to please. It is of the essence of the contract between himself and the public. Every time he publishes a book, he has stationed himself in the marketplace, beaten a drum (however modestly), and put up a placard promising to please if the public will give him a chance.

The first duty of an author, then, is to find a public, and his second duty is to hold it. In the old days there used to be a maxim that there is always a public waiting for anybody who has anything to say that is worth saying; but I am quite sure that to make the maxim true today one must add this clause, 'if it is something the public wants to hear said'. Literary reputations are made more easily now than they were in the past; but they are also more easily lost. Twenty or thirty years ago a successful author was in a situation as comfortable as that of a respected shopkeeper to whose shop a sufficient number of customers came regularly year after year. Unless he did something outrageous he was secure in their custom, and need not dread the establishments on each side of him or the rivals across the way. That good time is gone. Today, he must work hard to retain his old customers, and harder still to gain new ones.

And there is no surer way of jeopardizing a reputation than by the mistake of giving the public what they do not expect or wish for at the moment of publication. Two or three such mistakes, if consecutive, will kill an author dead unless he is exceedingly strong and healthy. Young authors who have received sudden and generous favour ought to be particularly careful to avoid this danger. For it should be remembered that a book may be very good as a book, and yet be a disaster on the commercial side (the side of which I am speaking) because of its untimeliness. And further than this, one may note that the untimeliness can be of two kinds. The book may be either untimely in regard to general taste, opinion, feeling, or untimely in regard to the author's actual reputation and standing. . . .

Authors, especially young ones, should not be in too great a hurry to bring out their best things. There is danger in changing subject and manner early in a career. . . . A man's words never have their proper weight and values until many people have become accustomed to listening to him, and no teacher teaches so well as he who has insinuated himself into the confidence of his pupils by not appearing to have any lessons to enforce.

John Galsworthy

MY FRIEND MR MAXWELL says he does not 'understand the mental attitude of writers who say, apparently quite sincerely, that they write to please themselves and do not in the least care how many or how few readers they have'.

Now, there aren't any writers who quite sincerely say all that. There are writers – I am unashamedly one of them – who quite sincerely say they write to please themselves – of that more anon; but what such writers mean when they loosely add 'they don't care in the least how many or how few readers they have,' is simply that they don't intend consciously to go out of the only way in which they feel they can best write, in order to gain more readers. Every writer, of course, would like to be read by as many people as possible – that's commonsense and human nature; but the kind of writer Mr Maxwell says he doesn't understand – though I think he understands them really far better than he imagines – is persuaded that the best way in the end, even to gain readers, is to present his fancy, and life as he sees it, as sincerely and perfectly as he can, and trust to the intrinsic value of his presentation to make its mark with the public. In the long run I can assure young authors that this is the only way to secure a worthy public; and though he may not realize it, I feel quite sure it is the method Mr Maxwell himself has adopted. . . .

It is a naked and uncompromising truth that to assess the real great public's taste is quite beyond the power of any writer; he may discover formulas to suit a certain section of the public, and go on turning out an article to pattern; but that way lies rank mediocrity or worse. The real great public, the public of the future as well as of the present, can be reached only by a very single-minded attention, to doing the best work one can, guided by one's own conscience, and by the conscience of nobody else. . . .

For – consider! Of what does a writer form his work, if it is to have any value, or to please any one worth pleasing? Out of his own fancy and vision, his own first-hand observation of life and character, his own moods, his own temperament, all trained and tempered to economy and clearness by his own experiments with words. We are ever being educated by our own efforts and our own reading; but we do nothing but waste time if we dwell morbidly on whether this or that creation will please these or those persons of our acquaintance, which – mind! – is all we can really know of the public taste. I don't hesitate to say that a writer who flounders about, consciously groping for indications from other people of what will give him a market or a name, will never achieve a real name, and will never survive his own day; nor will he even attain the market value accorded to those of sterner stuff.

And then there is this to be considered: To talk of public taste as if it were a 'constant' is an absurdity; it is an ever-moving variant. But what varies it? Why! the writer. That is his duty and his privilege. It is he who moves on the public's taste in literature. With every real piece of literary creation public taste gets a fresh jolt; it alters just a little. No writer of sense, none with anything of the artist in him, attempts *consciously* to influence the public taste; but every sincere writer with any vision brings something into that pool, and helps to widen it. If this were not so, if public taste did not follow the writer, we should all to this day be confectioning our tales in the picaresque manner of Fielding and Smollett and others popular at the outset of the British novel. . . .

148

The advice I always give to young or would-be writers rash enough to ask me for any, is this: 'Don't trust to what you can make by fiction; if you have not independent means, however small, then have another job as well, which will enable you to live until your work – the best work you can turn out, the most satisfying to yourself – finds its legitimate place and price.' I think it's bad both for them and for literature that they should succumb to the demands of publishers, editors, or agents, for this or that kind of story. No one is bound to write fiction for a living unless it's the very best fiction, light or serious – according to his grain – that he can turn out.

Fiction is an important thing – whatever may be the view of those who suffer from it; one could go almost so far as to say that it's now more important to human society than reality, because, through fiction, most people experience at second hand far more than humdrum life gives them at first hand. Surely, then, those who write fiction ought to make the best fist they can of it, and must lose their self-respect if they don't.

Hugh Walpole

S<small>IR</small>, – I hope you will allow me a little space to protest against Mr W.B. Maxwell's extraordinary article in the January *Author*. I have for so long had so strong an affection both for Mr Maxwell and his work that the fact that he is the author of this article makes it difficult for me to reply; but I feel his doctrine to be so dangerous that I cannot keep silent.

His article rests on this statement: 'There is no surer way of jeopardizing a reputation than by the mistake of giving the public what they do not expect or wish for at the moment of publication.'

I assert, in reply, that there is no surer way of jeopardizing a reputation than by just that very attention to what the public wants. The public? What public? Can Mr Maxwell have published books for all these years without realizing that there *is* no public; without realizing that from the instant an author begins to consider whether this subject or that, this treatment or the other is likely to please the public, he is lost; for the very reason that this will-o'-the-wisp, the public, is for ever just out of his grasp, and that while he is attempting to please it he is inevitably losing that direct communion with his subject which is his only hope and his only joy?. . .

I risk the charge of priggishness when I say it is the happiness of the artist and the happiness of the artist only that is the writer's lasting reward. Of course every author cares that his work should be read, cares for the money that

150

his work brings him, for the friendships, the thanks for pleasure rendered, but these joys must not approach him, however vaguely, until his work is finished. While he is engaged upon it he must see only the work, and anything that comes between himself and it will deprive him of authenticity, sincerity, and all that marvellous experience that living in a world created by some power other than his own, although disciplined and controlled by his efforts, gives him.

The quality of Mr Maxwell's work is proof sufficient that he knows these things to be true.

Nevil Shute

In your Summer number Mr Arthur Calder-Marshall, reviewing an American book, has produced this little gem: 'The bestseller . . . gives an idea of what is read on the periphery of literacy, the reading matter of those who have graduated from the literature of the lavatory wall to the printed word.'

I have written a good many books which have sold in large numbers and, perhaps not unnaturally, I take a different view of the intelligence of the reading public. On three separate occasions, in 1938, in 1945, and in 1949, I have found myself with a large public for my books and with money enough saved to keep me for ten years. On each of those occasions I have made the decision to cash in on my popularity and slam down upon my public with a book that would have real social value, accepting the probability that my sales would decline heavily in consequence because it seemed to me to be a good thing to do. On each occasion I have written this book as a work of fiction in order to get the widest public for the things I wished to say.

On each of the three occasions that book has sold in larger numbers than anything else that I had written to that date. On each occasion the book was a selection of a major American book club. Your readers must put their own interpretation on those facts in the light of their own experience, but may I give my view?

In my opinion the readers of novels are far more intelligent than unsuccessful writers will believe. They are expert in detecting, and merciless to, the conceited author, and the insincere author, and the author with all the tools of literature at his command who has nothing to say worth reading. Most reviewers are unsuccessful practitioners of the art of creative writing or they would not be interested in the meagre fees they get for writing about other people's books, and in part their lack of success may be due to the fact that they have completely misunderstood the character and the intelligence of the reading public. Young authors should accept the embittered fulminations of reviews against that public with the very greatest reserve; from the nature of their employment these people are quite unlikely to know what they are talking about.

Bernard Shaw

FOR NEARLY TWENTY years I have been a published author, and, for nearly ten out of the twenty, one of the most insufferably beparagraphed public persons in the country. But I have never yet seen a book of mine offered for sale in a shop window. That a certain number of fanatical Shavians do, by dint of laborious inquiry and indomitable perseverance, manage to procure a sufficient number of copies of my works to make them worth publishing is true; but the ordinary non-Shavian Englishman knows no more of the existence of my books than he does of those of Samuel Butler, or Ruskin, or Wagner, or Weissman, or Ibsen, or Maeterlinck, or Murray's translations of Euripides, or anything else that is not 'pastime for all'. I happen to be specially dependent on the bookseller, because I write plays, and publish them mostly three to the volume; so that the purchaser who wants to get a particular play needs guidance as to what particular volume that play is in. In France, if you want to buy, say Labiche's *Cagnotte*, you can ask the bookseller which volume of Labiche's *Théâtre* it is in, and he will tell you, and probably have the volume in stock to hand to you. But suppose you have heard that one of my plays is called *Caesar and Cleopatra*, and you want to buy it. You go to the bookselling stationer. The moment he realizes that you do not want a photograph frame or five quires of notepaper for a shilling, his countenance falls. You ask for Shaw's *Caesar and Cleopatra*. He has not got it, but can

154

order it for you. Good. You then call on him at intervals for three weeks or a month, and are assured each time that negotiations are proceeding. At last he tells you that there is no such book. You say you are sure there is. He replies that the wholesaler who supplies him could get it if there was; so it must be out of print. What can you do but apologize for having troubled him, and buy some stationery to console him? You then write to one of the second-hand booksellers, whose catalogues you get from time to time, instructing him to procure you a copy. Three years later he informs you eagerly that he has at last obtained the offer of a copy in perfect condition, which he can let you have for a guinea. If you are an infatuated Shavian you send the guinea, and receive therefore a new copy of *Three Plays for Puritans,* which the stationer would sell you for four and sixpence net if only you were able to give him all the information which it is a bookseller's business to give you.

I need not labour the point further. What we want above all things is not more books, not more publishers, not more education, not more literary genius, but simply and prosaically more shops.

QUESTIONS OF
CENSORSHIP

From the recurrent articles in *The Author* on censorship and the obscenity laws we have selected an article by E.M. Forster (Spring 1934), an extract from Benn W. Levy (Summer 1938), an editorial (Autumn 1968) and a piece by John Mortimer (Summer 1970).

When you tell me that you have altered 'beastly' into 'inhumanly drunk'. . . I really think it is time for me to give up in despair.

Thomas Hughes (author of Tom Brown's Schooldays) *to Alexander Macmillan, from* Letters to Macmillan, *edited by Simon Nowell-Smith, Macmillan, 1967 (quoted Spring 1968)*

Bloody; courtesan; dago; eunuch; guts; gigolo (always censored in England); joint (referring to a brothel); lousy; lover (illicit sex term); mistress (illicit sex); pansy; punk; sex appeal; slut; tart.

From the list of words vetoed by the Hays Office in all talking pictures in the USA (quoted Autumn 1936)

THE CENSOR AGAIN?

E.M. Forster

AUTHORS CAN BE divided into left wing and right. It is a superficial division because it takes no account of the only thing which makes an author worth reading – his merits – but it is of practical convenience when questions of general policy are involved. The right wing usually votes conservative; it upholds the existing order, the official outlook, and the literary tradition, and it has done much service to authors as a whole by securing them recognition from the powers that be. We should not have our social position or our financial hopes but for the right wing. The left wing votes progressive; it innovates, criticizes, sometimes shocks, and often destroys, and it, too, has done much service to authors by keeping them in touch with change in a world which is always changing. We should have degenerated into a governmental department but for the left wing. On the right in England at the present day are some good writers, Rudyard Kipling among them, and many bad ones, and they are balanced on the left by some good writers, Bernard Shaw among them, and by many bad ones. Right or left, good or bad, we all belong or should belong to the Society of Authors, because in such matters as our relationship with publishers or literary agents we have a common interest, and we ought to hang together like any other trade union.

Our difficulties start and our ranks begin to waver when we pass from material things to some general question of opinion. Questions of opinion are not always general. For instance, if one writer dislikes another's work he can call it tosh without involving a third party, and he can expand his criticism into 'pernicious tosh' if he belongs to the right wing and into 'ungenerous tosh' if he belongs to the left without splitting our Society, which rightly looks with an equal eye upon such internecine strife.

However, a question of opinion becomes general when a book is condemned, or is likely to be condemned, by the law. When this occurs we are all concerned with the verdict, because we all write, and we cannot help looking to the Society for some lead. The state is not a literary institution, and its verdict on any particular book is a matter of general concern. Is the verdict just? Is it unjust? And what, in either case, are its repercussions on our business of writing?

The particular book which may before long be of general concern to us is a very famous book, Joyce's Ulysses.[1] A reputable firm of London publishers will probably attempt to publish Ulysses in this country, and it is desirable that authors, as a whole, should decide what line they will take up before the excitement starts, for there is bound to be some excitement. The left wing, with whom I associate myself, will certainly wish it published. What will be the attitude of the right wing? Will they dismiss it, unread, as filth or hot stuff? Or will they try to get hold of a copy and judge for themselves? It is a serious book, a difficult book, a depressing book. No one on the right wing could possibly enjoy it. But no one can possibly regard it as pornography if he reads it as a whole. It is a mirror of the twentieth century's unrest, and it is bound to get published sometime, if only for its value to the social historian. It is also an amazing assemblage of literary devices, into which

---

[1] Ulysses was first published in February 1922 by Sylvia Beach in Paris. Shortly before this article appeared in The Author Joyce's book was published by Random House in the United States. It was not until 1936 that it was published in Britain, by the Bodley Head, in a limited edition of 1,000 copies. The first trade edition followed in 1937. [Ed.]

no writer can look without finding some salutary caricature of his own method. And it is, possibly, a masterpiece.

This is the book which is in danger of being 'censored', to use the popular word. There is, of course, no actual 'censorship' of books. The process is more complicated and we had better prepare ourselves for what may occur. A complaint about *Ulysses* would be made, after its publication, to a police magistrate, and he, if he thought fit, would order all copies to be seized. Then he would summon the publishers to show cause why the seized copies should not be destroyed, and if, after hearing the case, he decided that the book was 'obscene' they would all be duly destroyed. And what makes *Ulysses* 'obscene'? The magistrate will have nothing whatever to guide him. He must, however much he desires to be impartial, yield to his personal reaction or to his vague idea as to what is expected from him by the public or the press. 'Obscenity' has never been legally defined. When the Act which the magistrate will administer – Lord Campbell's Act – came up for discussion in the House of Lords about eighty years ago there was much opposition. Its critics complained that it would throw too much responsibility on the magistrate, and they have been quite right. Shortly after it became law, Chief Justice Cockburn made a ruling on it, according to which a book is 'obscene' when it is likely to corrupt the mind of any reader who is liable to be corrupted. This is not very helpful, for neither the reader nor his mind can easily be brought into court. So the magistrate has to decide how he feels and hope for the best. At the time of *The Well of Loneliness* case, about forty authors went to Bow Street prepared to say that Miss [Radclyffe] Hall's book was not obscene – and I suppose we meant by that that though our minds were liable to corruption it had not corrupted them. But the magistrate very reasonably refused to hear us. He felt he knew more about obscenity than we did, and he followed his feelings. His verdict was final, because though there was an appeal from him to Quarter Sessions, the justices there were not allowed an opportunity of reading the book for themselves, for the reason that the authorities did not consider it 'appropriate or practicable' to supply them with copies.

Whether we are left wing or right we must agree that the Campbell Act is very unsatisfactory and the magistrate, like the author, would probably be thankful if it could be amended. One suggestion is that the law should limit his powers to the suppression of books which are sold as pornography to people who seek out and enjoy pornography. But for my own part I feel that the Law, when it pronounces upon literature, is usually wrong, for the reason that it has to judge a book by something that can be quoted from it rather than as a whole. As soon as a book comes before a magistrate it has very little hope of winning his approval, however much he may have admired it in his private capacity.

That is why I feel that if Mr Joyce's fellow authors want *Ulysses* to be published in this country they should say so now, and not wait until they are called into court, when they will do no good. His publishers will need all the help we can give them if they are not to be the victim of some journalist who wants to start a scandal in order to make his paper sell, and, through bad journalism, the victim of a bad law. We ought to do something at once. I should like to see a pronouncement from the Council of our Society saying that *Ulysses* ought to be published. And if, from reasons of policy, such a pronouncement is impossible, I should like the writers of the left wing to speak persuasively to their confrères on the right – perhaps in the columns of *The Author* – and to ask for their help in what is a matter of general concern.

A FREE THEATRE

Benn W. Levy

A FEW YEARS ago Mr E.M. Forster, writing in *The Author*, reawoke the eternally dormant question of literary censorship. He confined himself to novels; primarily to one novel in particular, *Ulysses*. There can have been few dramatists who were not stirred to envy at this reminder of the comparative rarity of novelists' provocation. *The Well of Loneliness* and then a few years pass: *The Sleeveless Errand*, more years; *Bessie Potter*. . . . And on each occasion there is a storm of influential protest that I dearly covet for my own branch. But for us interference is not the rare exception, the occasional accident precipitated by a disreputable newspaper stunt: it is the rule. The blue pencil (or the submission to it) for each and every play, a complete ban for many.

Now the anomaly is that in a land where every smallest trespass upon freedom of expression raises a righteous and usually effective storm of protest and resentment, we acquiesce in, and some of us can sometimes even be found to support, conditions for the drama which are basically indistinguishable from the conditions that shock us so much in contemporary Germany and Russia.

Why is this discrimination against the theatre? The counterpart of Low's mildest cartoon would not be allowed on the stage, though at least 95 per cent more people would see it in an evening paper than in the theatre. Why is a writer forbidden to say in the form of a play all the things that he is allowed to say in the form of a novel, an essay, a biography, a travel book or a newspaper article? But – biggest 'why' of all – why are we not shocked into seeing that this injustice, this ugly exception to the particular English tradition of which most English people are proudest, should be removed? It is not the concern of dramatists only. I burn indignantly with Mr Forster when his trade suffers its relatively rare repressions. Will he and his colleagues not burn with me a little at the repression which is the permanent condition of mine? We can do with their help.

The reasons for our unrebellious submission to this yoke are manifold. We are used to it: it existed before any of us were born: we don't even know what it is like to participate in a free theatre. Furthermore, a long series of abortive attempts to secure one has made each fresh attempt seem stale, dull and unprofitable. The subject's become boring. It has acquired the unreality of King Charles's head.

Moreover there is certain vested opposition. Managers are frequently supposed to support the present system on the grounds that it insures them in advance against the costly accident of a police court prosecution and possible closing down of their show. I cannot think, however, that this pusillanimous view is very widely held, for the example of America indicates that the danger is not substantial and that managers would gain enormously on balance through the consequent accession of vitality to the theatre.

Again, a Bill to emancipate the theatre would rally only the most disinterested Parliamentary support, for it could bring its partisans no votes in the country. It has even been judged likely to lose them some among that hypothetical section of the electorate ridden by what is perhaps libellously considered to be the Nonconformist conscience and who could be easily convinced that such a bill was designed to promote the most licentious aspects of the Roman Empire in its decline; a form of argument invariably trotted out whenever any extension of liberty is under discussion.

Another very potent force acting against reform has been

the personnel and conduct of the Lord Chamberlain's Office under Lord Cromer. The Censor's task is unique and impossible. He is shot at from all sides and has neither statutory nor case law to shelter behind; nothing but his own arbitrary and personal judgement. Unfortunately Lord Cromer and his colleagues have somehow contrived to carry this preposterous task with so much courtesy, toleration, sympathy, patience and understanding that they have succeeded in minimizing the provocation of their anomalous autocracy. . . .

Perhaps the most powerful reason of all for our apathy is that censorship is a bondage that doesn't really seem to matter very much. Are its consequences really very serious? Many people do realize, of course, that the consequences of any unnecessary bondage whatever are extremely serious, whether visible to the naked eye or not. But these may not be sufficiently numerous or organized to secure action. For the others, the banning of plays or of passages in them is too remote and usual an occurrence to be dramatic. Also (unlike a banned novel) it lacks the publicity of a court case. . . . There is nothing but a quiet routine execution behind closed doors. And that execution, says the layman, what does it really amount to? A few lines cut or altered; or, at worst, the author told to go home and write another play. The thing is important to him perhaps, but to nobody else.

But it is of importance to other people . . . the theatre is not respected; it is regarded with condescension, with indifference, with an easy-going contempt. It is taken lightly because the shackles upon it have trained it to take itself lightly. Its staple diet, as Mr Ivor Brown recently observed in a painfully accurate phrase, is 'tiny comedies about tiny people'. Its audiences, as a result, have been thinned down to people who desire only that fare and will keep away when anything else is offered. The public that awaits and rewards the serious novelist has been taught that the theatre has nothing for them. For so long our audiences have been accustomed to a theatre which has been forced by censorship to empty itself as far as possible of all thoughtful, that is to say controversial, material that they do not readily accept it now, even when the ingenuity of dramatists succeeds in presenting it in a form innocuous to the Censor.

BY ANY OTHER NAME . . .

Editorial

No AUTHOR *wants* to be censored, although some perceive a need for keeping *other* writers under control. And nobody who does the censoring (outside the offices of the British Board of Film Censors) readily owns up to it: censorship is usually described by some less emotive term, such as guidance, editing, frank criticism, commonsense advice – a helpful, neighbourhood activity. On television it is sometimes called postponement. Even the Lord Chamberlain's men, whose vetoes were more clearly visible than those of the national watchdogs in other media, distastefully rejected the noun: what they had been doing for 200 years, they insisted, was *licensing*. But whatever name is given to the process, the result, for the writer, is the same: an interference with his freedom which is often damaging and almost always unwarrantable.

In many different ways, and under different names, censorship seems to be an inseparable condition of authorship, even in a society as relatively open as Britain; the closer an author approaches the moral nerve-centres of his society, the greater is his occupational risk. And although the majority of British writers may never be exposed to *official* censorship of any kind, *unofficial* censorship is going on all the time, here and there, by publishers, printers, librarians, booksellers, television executives, film producers and magazine editors. All that writers can hope to do is to achieve the maximum

167

possible freedom, within the law; and to be alert to those restrictive practices which aim to reduce it.

The most serious problems of censorship, in our view, concern religion, politics and violence; and the relative scarcity of argument about the first two of these areas should not be taken to imply that there is no threat to the writer's freedom to explore them. During the recent investigation into theatrical censorship, it emerged plainly that the Lord Chamberlain's Office had attempted to modify or even veto productions because of their political content; and it is in the field of contemporary political comment that the mysterious workings of television censorship have been most recognizable. Yet it is, traditionally, upon another area that the British debate always focuses and in which passions on either side are predictably aroused: the sexual and excretory functions of the human body, and the language in which writers are permitted to describe them, if at all.

AFTER THE CHAMBERLAIN

John Mortimer

THE THEATRES Act, 1968, has, with a few hundred somewhat laboured strokes of the pen, elevated the status of
theatre writers from that of the lowest lackey at the Court of
St James to the most carefully protected of all public
performers. Dramatists are now free to write about the
Church, the Royal Family, recent history and contemporary
politics. Producers of plays cannot be prosecuted without
leave of the Attorney-General, but they may find that the
Law Courts face them with a more bleak and unfriendly
world than the cosy jocularity of Lord Cobbold's office. So far,
a wise and tolerant Attorney-General has not licensed any
theatre prosecution. But no doubt with a new government
and an increasing Puritan reaction, prosecutions may come,
and it is well that we should be prepared for the worst.

The English law of obscenity contains one supposedly
progressive statute, the Obscene Publications Act, 1959, and
a dark wilderness of bye-laws and far-reaching restrictions,
mainly conceived in the middle of the last century. The
journalist, the artist and the photographer are subject to
such diverse laws as the Post Office Act, the Indecent
Advertisement Act and the Town Police Causes Act, which
put him at risk if he displays or sells any 'indecent' material
or sends it through the post. The word 'indecent' is well
calculated to allow the most backward tribunal to vent its
most archaic prejudices. It has been defined quite recently
by the Lord Chief Justice as that which 'offends the decency

169

of the average man'. No one knows who the average man is, except that he is invariably someone else. In the 1930s a Scottish judge defined indecency as, for instance, 'the conduct of a man who undressed in the presence of lady bathers'. With this handy definition most art galleries could be closed by Mr Callaghan if he put his mind to it, as he probably will.

These inconvenient bye-laws have been excluded from operation on the play producer by the Theatres Act, and the test of obscenity in the theatre is now exactly the same as it is in the Obscene Publications Act, 1959. The magic words provide that a play or book is not to be held obscene unless it has a tendency to deprave and corrupt; and in the *Last Exit to Brooklyn* case the Court of Appeal said that it must be shown to tend to deprave and corrupt a significant number of those likely to read or see it. The wording of the 1959 Act is not new, but imported from a mid-nineteenth-century case (*R. v. Hicklin*), decided at a time when skirts were being made for piano legs and the counsel engaged in the case was able to ask, 'What could be more obscene than the Venus in the Dulwich art gallery?'

In the *Last Exit* case, the Court of Appeal made it clear that the Obscene Publications Act narrows the definition of obscenity and confines it to that which has a tendency to deprave and corrupt. In theory, therefore, plays which the Court merely finds shocking or revolting or disturbing should not be found to be obscene unless a corrupting tendency can be proved. No one has ever defined what the sinister phrase might mean, and the Court of Appeal has said that it is a matter for the jury to decide in any particular case. Not only does the unfortunate jury have to do this without any legal guidance, but they are not allowed to hear any evidence on the subject. Experts can be called on the literary or social merit of the work, but are not allowed to say whether they think it would have a tendency to deprave or corrupt; as this is the question for which the jury are expected, as if by magic, to dredge up an answer from the dark recesses of their mind. When Sir Basil Blackwell, an elderly Oxford bookseller, attempted to tell the court that he had never felt quite the same since he read *Last Exit* the evidence was later said to have been inadmissible, and the alarming details of Sir Basil's change in personality were, perhaps happily, never investigated.

Although the law is fairly clear on the matter, in practice it is very difficult for a jury not to decide cases on the ordinary, everyday meaning of the word 'obscenity'. It is very difficult for a layman to disregard his instinctive feelings of shock and disquiet and substitute for them an academic concern for the moral welfare of a hypothetical group of people. The truth is that the word 'obscenity' is not one which can be given a practical legal definition, or mean much more than what an individual judge or juror may happen to find distasteful.

The Theatres Act also borrows from the Obscene Publications Act the defence of public good. A play is not to be condemned if its obscenity is outweighed by its artistic, social or other merit. The defence of public good, brought in in 1959 as a triumphant victory for the forces of progress, provides the law with a conception of mind-bending obscurity. The jury must first find a play or a book obscene, that is to say that it must tend to deprave and corrupt those unfortunates submitted to it, and then go on to be satisfied that the corruption of a wide number of persons is in the public interest because of literary or other merit. It is small wonder that this is an idea that few judges have been able to explain or juries to grasp; and the procession of novelists, sociologists, lady welfare workers and enlightened bishops who are ever prepared to give evidence as to 'public good', has never done much to deter a jury from condemning a book or play they found shocking in the first place.

Apart from the defence of public good, the play producer has the additional protection of the provision that no prosecution can be brought against a play without the leave of the Attorney-General. There is no doubt that this is a most valuable provision, the present ugly rash of petty prosecutions under various branches of the obscenity law having been instigated by the local police.

The risks of abolishing the Lord Chamberlain were well known and taken with calculation. An impossibly arbitrary nanny has been dismissed, and the theatre must now be prepared to face the so-called adult world of the British law courts. We must expect to find there juries who have never read a book or been inside a theatre, and a judge whose most modern literary experience may have been the televised version of *The Forsyte Saga*. Courtroom dialogue between the contemporary writer and those charged with his fate may, in these circumstances, be difficult and the results of future trials under the Theatres Act are uncertain.

This is not to say the Act is not a step forward. A democratic process, subject to public scrutiny and appeal, has been substituted for an autocratic censorship. However, the next step must be reached as soon as possible. The Arts Council Working Committee has recommended, and the Theatre Enquiry has supported, the removal of all legal censorship. Contrary to the belief of some, the Arts Council Committee did not start out predetermined to abolish censorship; the Committee started by trying to improve the law. Quite late in our deliberations it became obvious that no amount of progressive goodwill can produce a workable obscenity law, and whether or not a play is obscene is simply not a question which a law court is equipped to decide. There is only one tribunal for obscenity, individual taste; only one punishment, refusal to buy a ticket.

• • • •

You cannot find a better police for literature than criticism and the author's own conscience. People have been trying to discover such a police force since the creation of the world – but nothing better has been found.

Anton Chekhov (quoted Autumn 1968)

THE ONE NECESSITY

Two aspects of the writer's greatest need – time – were discussed by Sir Victor Pritchett in Spring 1978 and by Paul Tabori in Autumn 1969.

An author has perhaps two periods when he is happy, and they do not last very long. The first is when he is contemplating a new book, but has not really begun to work on it, and is sitting smoking his pipe . . . and then the time comes to settle down to work and that happiness has gone. The second period is when, for a moment after the work is done, you feel as if a great load has been lifted from your shoulders, and you see . . . in that muddle of manuscript something unique, something created once and for all; but then the manuscript goes away to the publishers and printers, and you begin to wonder about it. Hope departs, and with the arrival of the proofs despair returns. . . . All the rest of an author's life, I am afraid, is vexation and vanity.

J. B. Priestley, speaking at the annual dinner of the Society of Authors, Winter 1930

For forty-odd years in this noble profession
I've harboured a guilt and my conscience is smitten.
So here is my slightly embarrassed confession –
I don't like to write, but I love to have written.

From 'My Sin' by Michael Kanin, originally published in the Dramatists Guild Quarterly, *New York (quoted Autumn 1979)*

SPARE TIME

V.S. Pritchett

IT IS WELL KNOWN that, when two or three authors meet, they at once start talking about money – like everyone else. In fact, authors are not really talking about money at all; they are talking about *time*. For them time is the one necessity of their lives, not simply for high jinks – everyone has that – but time for their particular work. Productivity is natural to them, almost a kind of illness. They are born non-strikers. There is no book of any quality that is not the result of overtime, of productivity without bonus. The book you read in a few hours, days, or return to for weeks, has taken years to write and years of thinking before that. A writer, like all intellectual or creative workers, lives in two kinds of time – the clock time of his prose factory and the vitally necessary unending time of reflection; without the latter his work that clocks in will be dead and automatic. That indispensable reflective time has also to be bought nowadays and at a high price.

What is this time? In his young days Keats made a famous definition. He invented the term 'negative capability'. All writers have positive capability: they can fill their page, good, bad or indifferent. They assert their mind or self of the moment: but in order to reach that moment they have, like the actor, to annul the self, in order to become other characters, to become new selves. A writer must have the capacity to become passive and lost in doubt in order to be open to new suggestion. He must alternate between clocking

175

in and clocking off. It is this mysterious phase that is less and less possible in contemporary life, in which only immediate productivity is considered to be morally desirable. Yet in simple terms what writers call 'spare time' is hard to get. Only a tiny minority of authors can live on the money they earn from their books; the rest must have salaried jobs or turn to journalism in order to survive two new enemies: inflation and heavy taxation.

I have always been an independent writer because – providing one was willing to be relatively poor for much longer than most professionals are, and to live a kind of gambling life by one's wits – this was not difficult when I was young. In old age I see that to be self-employed is an anachronism – trade unions dislike us intensely. But I have survived by overwork. I do not repine nor am I, I hope, either proud or overweening about this, for I recognize that I am one of those neurotically anxious beings who are slaves of the 'work ethic' and that this may even show. By temperament I am a perpetual writer and like others of my kind I put in a good twelve-hour day, writing or reading in order to write, pretty well every day of the week. (I write this on Christmas Day.) I certainly work harder – as most elderly writers do – than when I was young. I agree that it would be more sensible if I left England for a country in which I didn't spend half the week working for the Inland Revenue. If I were to become enormously successful I might well leave the country, even though many writers lose something vital to their work when they uproot themselves from their native environment. But I am not rich and, since I have no 'spare time', I have to preserve my 'negative capability' as best I can.

The question must be put to the masters whom we cannot equal, especially those who were perpetual writers: say, Defoe, Richardson, Balzac with his sixteen-hour day, Dickens with his vast flow, Henry James who never stopped. The last three were men of great energy who, when they finished the day's stint, wrote dozens of long letters to their friends; ink poured out of them. If they travelled, they did so to write. I conclude they carried their 'negative capability' about with them all day and night whether they were dining out, thinking of more fantastic ways of piling up stimulating debts (Balzac) or bubbling over with self-communings like Henry James. Possibly their only time off for 'negative capability' came in their breakdowns or their ill-health; possibly also in those flat hours when they stood looking glumly out of the window, cleaned out their pipes, or like the tormented Dickens simply prowled the streets in the night: night-walking is valuable. In later years Kipling took to motoring as a way of taking in landscape and place – his special interest – as a narcotic. But, as far as self-renewal is concerned, I am pretty sure that what stirred their negative capability was the habit of writing.

Many a novelist has said he 'lets his characters take over'; or that not until he has written a few dull pages has his invention or imagination awakened. Often not until writing the third or fourth draft of a story do many writers discover their plot or theme. Perhaps for the perpetual writer the blessed 'negative capability' does not bring out its gifts until he has sloughed off his mechanical dullness in dozens of wasted pages. Always suspicious of 'inspiration', he understands that this hallucinatory state does not make advances to one as girls or handsome lovers do in erotic dreams, but has to be worked for.

A professional writer like myself has to learn to be a strategist in buying time for doing long things by getting through short ones. Edmund Wilson perfected this system by making the short ones tend to the themes of the long ones; still, he wrote no fiction after *Hecate County*. (He also did not pay his income tax for years and was caught and heavily fined. I do not recommend this.) The biographies I have written have eaten up a vast amount of my time. To write short stories one has to be something like a breeder and trainer of racehorses. They need months of veterinary attention – pages and pages of notes – and one is lucky to back a winner. Better for a short-story writer to be a restless doctor and small farmer like Chekhov than a literary critic. A doctor is forced to leave the house.

I find that reading Russian novelists, mainly of the nineteenth century, is good for my 'negative capability' – a state, incidentally, that means a state of vagary, doubt and indecision as well as self-annulment. I get pleasure for its own sake out of Gibbon on an idle Sunday evening; also from classic works of travel. If I work hard it is partly to offset a lazy mind. Painters taught me to love landscape. In London or if I chance to stay in the country I stand staring out of the window at the trees or garden. Gardening is good for writers: pruning and weeding are like proof-correcting. I like sleeping an hour or so in the afternoons. I like doing the local shopping in Camden Town: one hears such strange remarks. If I go abroad for a short time I prefer those countries in which I understand the language and am vain of being able to speak it. I take my work with me, but never do it. I like those countries where so much is lived in the streets, not behind the closed doors of northern Europe. Teaching in America has once or twice given me a lot of free time for work of my own – Americans are far more generous to writers than the British are. I mean in the matter of time, though I must say I am humbled by academic society: perhaps that is good. But lecturing is exhausting; and so are appearances on television: a writer should not live by his mouth.

I suppose, since I work alone and do not see many people – visitors are the writer's worst plague – I find conversation the most reviving of spare-time pleasures, for good conversation stirs up fantasy. One is startled to hear oneself saying things that one had no idea were in one's mind. I am not sure that I don't get more out of being near the vast spare time of others than I do out of my own, though I am horrified by the savage things the world nowadays finds time to do.

THIEVES OF TIME

Paul Tabori

WHEN I WORKED IN Hollywood, one of my best friends was
an extraordinary character whom I might as well call Peter
King. He was a writer who hated writing; a cynic who
constantly acted the Good Samaritan; a coruscating wit who
looked like a particularly depressed bloodhound. His main
occupation was that of script doctor; he seldom initiated any
creative work himself, but whenever a producer or a television
series were in real trouble, they sooner or later appealed to
Peter King. And whenever this happened and he was invited
to lunch at the Brown Derby or Chasen's, for dinner at the
producer's home in Bel Air or Malibu Beach, he always
asked the same question:

'How much conversation money?'

Nor would he accept any summons, however august, until
this particular point was settled. He wasn't greedy – a couple
of hundred dollars was his standard fee, for which he would
listen and perhaps even speak a few sentences. But people
had learned to respect this quirk, which hid a very deep
wisdom.

For Peter knew that a writer basically had only two things
to sell: time and ideas. And while he appeared to have an
inexhaustible supply of the latter, time was much more
precious. He had worked out that in a lifetime there were
only so many heartbeats and he refused to waste them –
unless he was paid.

I often think of Peter King. And I wish that his simple

question would be considered seriously and in detail by the Society of Authors and other professional organizations. The thieves of time are greater enemies of a writer than even plagiarists or pirates. For they are stealing his irreplaceable and most precious possession, his very life.

A few months ago a British film producer telephoned me. He had looked me up in some professional reference book, he knew something of my work and he wanted to discuss a screenplay. His name was unfamiliar but he mentioned two or three pictures with which he had been associated and I invited him for a drink. He had apparently bought a book by one of our most prolific, multiple-pseudonymed authors and wanted me to do a shooting script based on it. I told him what my usual fee was and he seemed to find it reasonable. I read the book, which was not one of the master's best efforts; to turn into a film would have needed a good deal of work in plot and character development. We had two or three meetings with the producer who was much excited by the ideas I developed. Then there was silence – and finally a letter saying that he couldn't quite meet my price and would I please return the book.

He was just as much a thief as if he had picked my pockets. He stole at least fifteen good working hours – never to be recovered.

Not long afterwards I received a letter from a reputable publisher. He wanted a book to be written on a historical subject of his own choice. I prepared a synopsis and we signed a contract. We discussed the project in great detail, but when I turned in the first 20,000 words it became evident that his ideas were totally different from mine; not only did he want the kind of book which I wouldn't write but one that couldn't have been written without the serious danger of libel. So we abandoned the project. The next I heard was a demand for the return of the advance. I pointed out that there was nothing in the contract to justify such a request, and that it hadn't been my fault that he hadn't been able to formulate his conception of the book at the right time or communicate his ideas to me until it was too late. In the final analysis he, too, had stolen valuable time – for the book was never published and the advance certainly did not cover the many hours I had spent over it. I heard nothing more from him – but again, I had to add him to my short but constantly growing black list.

For I think that we should all establish our own black lists – various writers' organizations have actually done so – and should take protective measures against the thieves of time. The publishers who hang on to a manuscript for many months, returning it tea-stained and dog-eared; the editors who do not answer letters, or barricade themselves behind secretaries when they are afraid or ashamed to give a straight answer; the producers who have the mystic belief that the seventeenth script must be seventeen times better than the first one; the television moguls who demand an incredible amount of work 'on spec' because they are terrified of the responsibility of commissioning something even from perfectly professional, experienced writers – all these should go on our lists and they should be made available to any enquirer in some central place. No one would dream of going into a butcher's shop, asking for a leg of lamb and telling the man in the apron: 'I'll pay you for it when I have tried it and found it palatable!' No one expects the bricklayer to build a wall with the proviso that, unless it pleases the customer, he won't get paid for it. These are perhaps crude and not exact parallels but there is no profession in which so much brain-picking, so many confidence tricks, so much downright dishonesty are perpetrated at the expense of the creative artist.

CRITICS AND REVIEWERS

This teasing subject is a hardy perennial in *The Author*'s columns, where several symposia have been devoted to it. We take our extracts from the Summer 1943 forum, 'Reviewing Reviewed' (E.M. Forster, Bernard Shaw, St John Ervine); John Bowen's 'Reviewers and Reviewing' (Spring 1972); and Paul Jennings's '500 Words if You're Lucky' (Summer 1970).

To review a book without having read it . . . is not criticism. It is obtaining money under false pretences.

To review a book without cutting the leaves, by dipping into it here and there, is not criticism. It is laziness.

To review a book by writing a paragraph which reproduces the plot of the book is not criticism. It is petty larceny.

To hold a brief against a book, and to review it by picking out every weak passage, and holding it up to ridicule without a word upon the other side, is not criticism. It is an aggravated assault.

To review a book anonymously in several papers, so that it appears that all these papers have independently come to a conclusion, when really it is only one man who has done so, is not criticism. It is impersonation.

But, in spite of all drawbacks, our critical press is, I think, better than any other critical press; and if a man is blamed where he does not deserve it now and then, it is morally certain that he will also be praised where he does not deserve it occasionally; and so the balance is adjusted.

Arthur Conan Doyle in the Morning Leader (*quoted January 1893*)

E.M. Forster

THE ETHICS OF reviewing depend upon the age of the reviewer. If he is mature, and of established position, he ought to be careful of what he says about his contemporaries, and still more careful of his references to his juniors. He is listened to because he has a name, he can influence his readers for that reason, and though praise is permissible (we none of us praise enough, as our President has reminded us), he should be chary over blaming. I can remember the later review work of Andrew Lang: his belittling of Joseph Conrad who was at that time obscure, and his implacable pursuit of Anatole France through magazine after magazine, because they differed on the topic of Joan of Arc. It was impressive at first. It ended by becoming depressing. And I can think of more recent and equally deplorable displays. On the whole, if an eminent reviewer feels that he is losing his temper with an author, he had better take the dog out for a walk; he may be calmer by the time he comes back. And he should be particularly cautious before he abuses the young, for ten to one he does not understand what they are trying to do.

The young reviewer, on the other hand, is entitled to laxer standards. If he wants to hit out at his seniors, or even at his contemporaries, he has a right to do so. I used to do so when I started writing, and can still recall with pleasure the dressing down I gave pompous old Sir Sydney Lee. Of recent years I have been dressed down myself, and have

185

indeed been described as a third-class novelist and low in my class. I thought the description was untrue. But I realized its propriety. For unless there is plain and even angry speaking on the part of young 'irresponsible' reviewers the academic corridors will never get aired, and literature will be stifled.

If the ethics of reviewing depend upon the age of the reviewer its content depends upon the space allotted to the review. Most reviews today do not exceed a couple of hundred words and there is only room to describe the nature of the book, its aims, its success in achieving those aims, and its chances of pleasing the public. Given a thousand words or more the reviewer can go in for being clever or learned and attempt criticism. But his first duty is to say what the book is about and whether it will be liked.

Some reviews give pain. That is regrettable, but no author has any right to whine. He was not obliged to be an author. He invited publicity, and he must take the publicity that comes along. . . . He would be wise to ignore attacks upon his literary reputation, however monstrous and malicious they may be. Only his writing can look after his writing. Nothing else can defend it. No amount of damages or of apologies in court can make it one word the better.

Bernard Shaw

Among the drudgeries by which the aesthetic professions
have to save themselves from starvation, reviewing is not the
worst. . . . Even so, it is, like gathering samphire, a dreadful
trade. I earned my first income in literature by practising it.
And I found that eminent authors were still slaving at it as
publishers' readers to make both ends meet. I began, some
sixty-four years ago, by doing what every beginner in
literature did then; I wrote novels, useful enough to myself as
'prentice work, but all unanimously rejected by the publishers.
The appalling part of the business was that among those
who had to read my novels for the publishers were George
Meredith and John Morley. Meredith vetoed me without
apology; Morley took me for a young man whose head was
turned by Ruskin, and wrote about me at such length that
George Macmillan softened his firm's refusal by sending me
a copy of John's report.

Imagine authors of their standing having to read my
jejune fictions for a living! I have often wondered how much
they got for the job from Macmillan and Chatto. The usual
fee for a publisher's reader at that time was supposed to be a
guinea per book; but later on I found a lady with a quite
respectable literary talent reading books for half a crown.

I never acted as publisher's reader; for when I had written
five novels in five years without getting one of them
accepted, on the advice of these most important (to us
authors) of all reviewers I earned my first regular money in

literature as reviewer on the old *Pall Mall Gazette*, edited by William Stead, who, though an expert in newspaper politics, was in literature and art a complete ignoramus (quite a usual combination still). I was paid £2 per thousand words. I acted also as picture critic for *The World* under Edmund Yates, mostly in paragraphs at 5d a line. Yates was genuinely horrified when I told him afterwards that by doing all the London picture exhibitions for him I had earned only £30 a year.

Later on, when a local paper owned by Lloyds suddenly blossomed into the *Daily Chronicle*, and became a leading London daily, I reviewed for it, and, to my great indignation, was offered remuneration at the rate of so much (I think it was 3½d) per compositor's 'stick'. I flung this back in the face of the reigning Lloyd, denouncing him as a sweater, and demanding £3 per thousand with a minimum of £5. This was considered so monstrous that Lloyd, a most benevolent man, I believe, was seriously upset by it; and even my friends H.J. Massingham and Henry Norman, then on the editorial staff, sympathized with him, and agreed that I should never again contribute to the paper. However, I did contribute, and on my own terms. It was a successful stroke of literary trade unionism.

I give these figures because I am writing as an author for authors in the journal of our profession. People who revile reviewers never ask themselves what they can expect for the little we poor devils, the submerged tenth of the upper ten, are paid for our drudgery. They get amazingly good value for their money.

Still, reviewing is hard on novelists. Novelists are not normal human citizens. They work all by themselves in an imaginary world which they create and arrange for themselves without interference or contradiction or remonstrance or criticism; and when the results are published and reviewed, not with unmixed and delighted assent but with criticism, dislike, or even coolness by the reviewers, they are outraged, and take the review as a corrupt personal attack. But if they don't like it they must lump it; for if they are not reviewed they will not get published. Novelists must learn to live in the real world as well as the *pays de Cockaigne* if they would escape making fools of themselves and belonging to a sweated profession instead of to a powerfully organized one. As it is, they hate organization, resent the protective inter- ference of the Society of Authors, and, if elected to a committee, behave like hogs.

The reviewers, on the other hand, find it overwhelmingly to their interest to please the publishers, please the authors, please everybody, and never get their editors into trouble, be it only the trouble of reading splenetic letters. Only critics of irresistible vocation find fault. They also make reviews readable. Most reviewers, fortunately for the authors, are complaisant newsmen, earning an irregular and insecure living by describing, as interestingly as they can, the latest books in the market. I, an old reviewer and a long-sufferer from adverse criticism, pity them and bless them.

St John Ervine

AUTHORS MUST BE THE only craftsmen in the world who have to submit to the criticism of inexperienced or incompetent people. A surgeon is not obliged to listen to the complaints of a student walking the wards for the first time, nor is he subjected to the rebukes of men whose patients have all perished under their knives. The Master of the Rolls would feel considerably surprised if his decisions were subjected to the scrutiny of a law student who has still to pass his finals, and he would resent it if he were obliged to defer to the revisions of a barrister whose clients were always convicted. The Archbishop of Canterbury would not, I feel, take it well if a divinity student or even a deacon told him where he got off. But no one thinks it odd that a lad who has succeeded with some difficulty in getting an article into *Granta* should instruct a Hardy or a Shaw, or that a person whose novels have been well pulped or whose plays have had their notices put up during the dress rehearsals, should criticize, not only with asperity, but with condescension, such authors as these. . . .

John Bowen

INSTANT CRITICISM IS A contradiction in terms. Criticism should be considered; reviewing must be done at once. The space allotted to reviewing would be insufficient for criticism, which is found in books and long, learned articles: worse, it (and consequently the review) is often reduced by sub-editors, who are inclined to remove the last sentence of every paragraph to make the copy fit the reduced space. Reviewing is catholic. . . . Criticism is specialized and exact.

Most importantly, the difference is of function. The critic evaluates, places, analyses; the reviewer responds. Response is important: it is not ignoble to be litmus paper. Where in the seventies reviewers have lost their influence, and done harm where they meant to do good, it is because they have forgotten the importance of response, have thought in terms of a higher duty to encourage what is serious, and particularly what is experimental, have forgotten or glossed over the warning that to be 'serious' is not the same as to be good, praised work for its intentions not its achievement, encouraged expectations in audiences and in readers which time and again have been disappointed, so that nowadays it may be enough for a play, book or film to be praised in certain terms by certain reviewers, for even 'serious' people to avoid it. Enthusiasm is part of response. A real enthusiasm is hard to fake, but the reviewer-who-would-be-critic, the reviewer-who-would-be-opinion-former becomes a stranger to enthusiasm. After a while, we may assume, he ceases to feel it.

Response is important, but it should be informed by knowledge. Eliot's dictum that, 'A critic must have a very highly developed sense of fact,' is as true for reviewers as for critics. . . . A reviewer of plays should know how plays are written, how rehearsed; at least enough about acting to tell what is flashy and selfish, what co-operative and controlled; enough about theories of acting and direction to know *why* what he sees is happening (even if he doesn't like it); at least enough about plays in performance to tell when something has gone wrong on the first night which may never go wrong again. The same knowledge of practice should be expected from a reviewer of novels, poems or films. If he should also have some knowledge of life and society – that is, of the raw material of literature, as well as the form – why, so he should, as we all should; but let him be careful, let him not confuse mere opinion with knowledge, or particular experience with general truth, and parade his own prejudices as facts.

Paul Jennings

I'm PRETTY SURE THAT no one, filling up a form, ever puts down under 'Occupation' the words *book reviewer*. In the government (HMSO) *Classification of Occupations*, a great thick book which attempts a kind of Dewey numbering of all the jobs done in Britain, from Easparto Potcherman to Head Splitting Operator, from Riddle Lad or Stage Whipper to Vaccination Officer or Final Inspector of Bullets, you will find, under 811 (Authors, Editors, Journalists, Publicists), a list of such trades as Dramatist, Caption Writer, Doctor of Literature, Turf Correspondent, Crossword Compiler, and of course Critic.

But not Book Reviewer. Of course Critic sounds altogether grander. It has a whiff of university respectability about it, with generation after generation of stern new *young* Critics telling us to rethink our attitude to Blake, to apply the dialectic to George Eliot, or whatever. It conveys the safe feel of criticism as an industry, of that splendid graffito seen in a New York subway, *boycott non-academic poetry*.

Yet a great deal of book reviewing gets done by people who would be almost as embarrassed to be called critics as ashamed to be called book reviewers. They are divided into roughly six classes, and if *they* aren't in the *Classification of Occupations* they ought to be: Bitcher, Batcher, Same Field Man, O-God Man, Hooray Man and B.H. Crumbhole Operator.

Perhaps because so many people in these classes write

various kinds of books themselves, and therefore have some rudimentary spark of feeling about the effort that goes into writing a bad book, just as much as a good one, there aren't all that many Bitchers. As far as I can see they operate most of all in the poetry field, and are often poets themselves (but this doesn't make a Bitcher a Same Field Man, which is an altogether wider category). 'Mr X's images are not so lambent as he imagines. This is wan stuff,' they say, or 'Mr Y's tightrope between Self and Not-Self turns out to be an umbilical cord firmly attached to the Self.' Or something.

Of course you very often get the occasional Bitcher throwaway line in, for instance, an O-God Man review (q.v.). 'Unfortunately Mr Z's contribution to these superb extracts consists largely of sociological cant.' But most book reviewers do not care, or dare, to have the full public image of Bitcher nowadays. They want to be loved.

Almost all writers, however, as literary pages get ever smaller and feature pages about abortion, drugs, lesbianism, men's toiletries, student problems, consumerism, fashion and advice, advice, advice get ever more copious, suffer from the Batcher. Of course *humorous* books have always been reviewed by Batchers, since no publisher would dream of bringing one out except at Christmas, when great piles of them are put on little tables near the bookshop door, as if to say to the weary shoppers, 'Come on in, don't be afraid, look, books are FUN, why not get one instead of bath salts for that old aunt.' So naturally they're reviewed in batches, by Batchers, probably the nearest to 'pure' Book Reviewers. There's always a weary sighing first paragraph. 'O God, here come the clowns again, tumbling in the sawdust with their painted grins. There is nothing more depressing than a pile of funny books. Do not, in this grey island, look for the acid wit of an S.J. Perelman (usually) . . . etc.' It's probably easier to do a Batcher review of funnies, though, than of five novels, since one will be about a blind negro pianist, one about lust in Widnes, one about an ageing chemistry

194

professor in a redbrick university who, tiring of his neurotic children, has an affair with his pretty young aunt and tries to build an idyllic new life with her in rural Wales, but there they meet a homosexual German farmhand, etc., one will be a Graham Greene reprint and one will be the new masturbation classic.

The Same Field Man is the commonest standby for reviewing non-fiction. As we have seen, although a Bitcher is very often a Same Field Man as well, the converse does not necessarily hold. A Same Field Man is more likely to be a Bitcher when reviewing anonymously, obviously. But usually he does a good useful job and limits his strictures to pointing out that the Treaty of Utrecht was in 1713, not 1317 and Mr A can't spell Caravvagio and why isn't there an index.

The O-God Man is the reviewer who is chosen after the literary editor, surveying one of those full-page-in-*Time-Magazine* books, such as *Games People Play* or the first Vance Packards, says, 'O God, who can we give *this* to?' I have been an O-God Man myself sometimes, usually with some dense, thought-packed, allegedly popularized scientific book, that an ordinary intelligent man is supposed to be able to understand. Once I met Anthony Burgess on a television quiz programme and discovered that we were both doing our nut on an admittedly fascinating book called *The Ambidextrous Universe* by Martin Gardner, all about spirals in crystal formation, and how you would relay information to another planet (non-visually) about which way round to wind an armature, and if there was nothing in the universe but a flat cardboard hand would it be a right or a left hand, and Madame Wu's experiment with cobalt-60, and the general possibility of a mirror universe. It was a week's intense work. On the jacket it said this was W.H. Auden's book of the year, but I think he was boasting. It wasn't W.H.Smith's, I bet, in spite of my underpaid swot. I don't know what they paid Anthony Burgess, but I got 20 gns., and I've only once got more than that (25 gns., there's wealth for you), for, such is the inequity of fate, doing a Hooray Man piece. This category is self-explanatory. As a matter of fact, though, now I come to think of it, that was a week's work too. Well, at least I'm never likely to become a Batcher at that rate (or rich).

A B.H. Crumbhole Operator is really a special version of a Same Field Man. When a book comes out with some title[1] like *Roadside Trees of Malaysia*, or *Scottish Lintels from 1700 to 1735*, or *Water-watches*, or *A History of Spandrels* there is very often this colossal expert, the world authority, who wrote some tremendous work on the subject. Either this man, who always has some name like B.H. Crumbhole, is very old, and gets the odd paragraph in a Sunday diary ('The Scottish Lintel Exhibition opens on Tuesday. Spry as ever, Mr B.H. Crumbhole . . .') or he is very young, and has set the Scottish lintel world by the ears at twenty-five. In either case he is the *automatic* choice for reviewing any work in his field. Usually he does the kind of review that is mostly an essay, with eighty non-committal words about the book right at the end.

I've left out three minor grades – Betcher (betcher I could do it better myself), Botcher and Butcher (no space left). I suppose most of us casuals – Hooray Men and O-God Men – only really do it because we can't think quickly enough to refuse on the telephone. But it makes things a bit more democratic. I don't think it should all be left to the Batchers.

---

[1] One of these four actually exists. Guess which.

WARTIME ATTITUDES

At an emergency meeting on 26 August 1914, reported in the October *Author* – no issues were published in August or September – the Society's Committee of Management 'begged to inform members' that from that time 'only the absolute essentials touching the work of the Society will appear in *The Author*, as it has been found necessary to reduce expenses as far as possible'. Partly for that reason, no doubt, one may search its columns in vain between 1914 and 1919 for any reflection of its members' attitudes to or experience of World War I, even for any indication that for many it meant the terminating not only of their contracts but also of their lives.

When World War II broke out *The Author* took a different attitude – partly because its editor, Denys Kilham Roberts, took a different view of the journal's function and also, perhaps, because of the changed attitude among British authors towards war itself. This was reflected in two successive symposia on 'Authors and the War', in Spring and Summer 1940, from which we have selected five of the following extracts. Four years later, in Autumn 1944, Squadron Leader H.E. Bates described his own rewards in uniform in the course of an article entitled 'The Rate for the Job'.

It not infrequently happens that publishers take advantage of the fact that an author is abroad, and in consequence do not deliver their accounts as regularly as they should.

Editorial, October 1917

... for bad writers to be wiped out might be as valuable to literature and country as for good ones to survive. But England cannot take the risk, *cannot* allow the good to perish with the bad. The writer can do far more for his country by writing than by fighting.

Sir Osbert Sitwell, Spring 1940

FREEDOM OF THE PEN

John Strachey

THE BEST THING THAT the government can do for authors in wartime is to leave them alone. The business of an author is to write. It is a painful and laborious process, and authors naturally make every attempt to evade it. They attempt to get jobs of all sorts in all kinds of ministries, etc. If they are political authors, like myself, they attempt, both in peacetime and wartime, to take on direct propagandist work, speaking, lecturing, standing for parliament, or what you will. That is all no good; or, rather, it is only good as a method by which an author can cease to be an author. That may be all to the good, both for himself and for the reading public. But it is not what is usually meant by the government helping authors.

However, there is an opposite side to the proposition that the government ought to leave authors alone, especially in wartime. Not only should it refrain from distracting them from writing by providing them with jobs in ministries; it should also allow them to write what they like, even if they do not agree with the government. In other words, the first and vital necessity for authors in wartime is that they should not be subjected to rigorous censorship. But, if the government should leave authors alone, this does not mean that authors should leave the government alone, in the sense that authors ought not to take an interest in public affairs or a part in public life in wartime. On the contrary, it is vital that authors should be active in two ways. In the first place

199

authors are one small but prominent section of the intellectual workers of the country. They are fully entitled to have their say in the national policy. They have their special interests as authors, such as the above necessity to watch out against the censorship in every possible way. Secondly, they can and should express their views on general national policy as citizens. Nor is it a contradiction to what I have said above to assert that authors will become far better authors if they take part in the national life in every possible way as individuals. For thus, instead of taking bogus jobs in this or that propagandist service, they will go through, as working individuals, the full experience of the nation. Hemingway, after having gone through a couple of campaigns, says that the first-hand experience of war is by far the most fruitful and useful thing that can happen to an author. It may well be that we shall have no need to be actually in the trenches to go through the full experience of violence during the course of this war; but whatever we do, whether it be fighting, making munitions, working on the land, or, on the contrary, engaging in one way or another in the struggles of the labour movement, we are likely to have some enriching experiences in the next year or so. Let us hope we benefit by them.

EXPLOITED PATRIOTISM

Bernard Shaw

WHEN WAR IS declared we all go mad. We assume that all who are doing anything must stop doing it and do something else, and that wherever we are we must go elsewhere. We forget, if we ever knew, that a war is only a ripple of slaughter and destruction on the surface of the world's necessary work, most of which must carry on without a moment's intermission, war or no war.

Now there is money to be made out of these insanities. In 1914, one of the first things that happened was that actors were asked to 'do their bit' by accepting half salaries for their work; and many of them, in an ecstasy of patriotism, did so, to the handsome profit of their exploiters. It was such a paying game that the said exploiters presently approached me with the proposal that 'of course' I would halve my fees for the duration. I replied that 'of course' I must double them, as the war would not only increase my income tax heavily, but the inevitable inflation and consequent rise in the cost of living would make a corresponding increase in my income a matter of life and death for me. In consenting, as I actually did, to make no change, I claimed credit for a heroic sacrifice, only possible for an author with some settled property at the back of his royalties. The exploiters were deeply shocked by my lack of public spirit, and set me down as an arrant pro-German. . . .

Most authors are as hopeless at business and economics as they are at mathematics. When war descends on them they do not sit down to a calculation of how it will affect their incomes: they feel romantic impulses to sacrifice and service which do credit to their feelings, but which end in their being gulled by unsentimental people who are sharp enough to see their chance and take it. . . .

Now far be it from me to restrain or discourage any author who gives what help he or she can in the emergency created by the war. Many authors think it an absurd and ruinous war, and have said so; but such declarations do not lessen the emergency. A conviction that the captain has scuttled the ship, or that his incompetent seamanship has wrecked it, does not make it less necessary to man the pumps. But throwing money into the sea will not help. On the contrary earning more money can. If I were to tell Sir John Simon that I had resolved to set an example of self-denial by allowing all my works to be published, performed, and filmed for nothing during the war, he would say, 'For heaven's sake do nothing of the sort. Screw every farthing you can out of your works and keep off the dole at all costs. Don't be afraid of your income being too big: my tax collector will see to that.'

The least the authors can do is to use their brains to avoid making themselves poorer for the benefit of the profiteer and the idle *rentier*. That is the way to impoverish their country, not to help it.

Also literature, being an artistic and learned profession, must be defended tooth and nail against the common Philistine presumption that fine art is an immoral luxury, and science and learning unpractical fads that must give way to the most trivial military considerations. Already the closure of schools, the seizure of cultural premises of all sorts to store munitions and accommodate military clerical staffs, and the stoppage of grants-in-aid to art are a scandal; and it is not reassuring to remember that in the last war the British Museum itself had a narrow escape of being commandeered for war work.

Evey day the Labour papers tell us of raised wages for our manual workers. When I hear of silly authors accepting less instead of demanding more, I wonder which of the two classes are the real brain workers, and which the congenital idiots.

THE AUTHOR'S DUTY

Henry W. Nevinson

THE FIRST DUTY OF an author in this war is to practise starvation. We have no paper to write on. Papyrus and wax tablets are antiquated. Parchment is beyond dreams. The forests of Finland and Russia, where I used to watch the fir trees hewn into lengths, carried far down torrents, caught by iron claws, torn into shreds, rolled and rolled again as in mangles, and hung up to dry, till they were almost as good as newspapers, except for the 'printed matter', which had to be added afterwards, then embarked on ships for London and other British ports – all those necessities of a writer's life have been 'liquidated'. Finland lies under Stalin's tyranny, Norway under Hitler's. The author's occupation is going, going. . . .

What, then, shall a writer do to be saved? A hundred to one he cannot dig. Two to one he is ashamed to beg. He must train himself in starvation until he can subsist on one meal a week. A boa constrictor with a kid bulging inside him will last him six months.

To be sure, if a writer is still under thirty-six or forty, he can join one of the three services, and probably that is the best thing he could do. He will be clothed for nothing in the 'battle-dress', hideous and uncomfortable, but still a 'suit'. Though bully beef and shackles are monotonous, they will keep him alive for the duration. If he is wounded, he will be tended by doctors and nurses free till he is fit to face fire again; and if he is killed, he will be celebrated as a genius cut off prematurely.

HOW TO KEEP GOING

Margaret Kennedy

No doubt it is a disaster that the intellectual production of a country should be brought to a standstill. Total war is an incomparable disaster. But in this respect, as in others, a country must draw on its resources. It must read old books, just as it wears old clothes. Fortunately books last better than clothes. Our nation would be in no real danger of intellectual malnutrition if no new books were published for five years. Enough has already been written to keep us going for some time, and if we really took pains to read our classics we might, after five years, have added to our mental stature.

Total war is not won by a brigade of authors. Attila waged total war, and won it, though he brought no novelists with him from his native steppes. He won it against cultured and civilized people, who, no doubt, continued conscientiously to 'create' until the city gates were broken down. Then all pens ceased. Not only were the books of the future doomed to be never written, but an incomparable heritage was destroyed as the books of the past blazed up in a thousand gutted libraries. The Huns have always been fond of burning books, especially books which have been greatly admired by civilized people for a long time. . . .

Meanwhile we have not yet got total war, though we are always being warned that it is just about to begin, or has begun already, like the millennium. Authors are still, many of them, free to maintain the nation's intellectual standards, just as many milliners are still free to trim the nation's hats.

205

They can write what they like, as they have done in former wars. And that is what most of them are probably doing. Some there are, to be sure, who complain that they can no longer write: the shock of finding themselves in such a violent and evil world has been too much for their nerves. But people as sensitive as this ought surely to have 'downed pens' some time before September 1939. Anybody who has been able to carry on imaginative work at all during the past two or three years must have developed a protective philosophy sufficiently tough to have sustained him through the past five months. There is no specific 'war time' in the modern world.

WAR OR REVOLUTION?

V.S. Pritchett

WHICH WAR AND what authors? Already the war has become a new war and seems likely to assume other and different forms before it is over. A large number of authors have not been affected by it mentally or materially at all. Each writer can only note his own reactions and circumstances. As reality becomes more fantastic and horrifying, many creative writers discover that their fictions seem more real and that it is easier to work; though the fact that we can live only from week to week makes it difficult to think out long-term projects. Possibly writers have started thinking; and certainly whether it is impossible to write or not impossible, now is the moment for thought! For example, is this a war? Is it not merely externally a war but really a social revolution? The first two victims of social revolution are freedom and economic security. Something might be done for the former by joining the Council for Civil Liberties; and for the latter, I think, writers should first provide themselves with literary agents and then see to it that these agents become public political figures instead of merely commercial brokers. Economically, the agent is the only figure behind whom the apparently fierce but actually timid and incompetent individualism of authors can really unite without having to admit it. Authors who foresee exile should get in touch with their friends in America and the colonies; and most should prepare to be poorer, especially that astonishing minority who live on either private incomes or their books. But those lucky enough to have the right views will as usual get richer. The real economic struggle is going to begin when popular publishing with a huge public finally destroys the gains in status and income which authors have had under the present system of restricted and expensive publishing. 'Think of the publicity' is no answer to low royalties.

THE RATE FOR THE JOB

H.E. Bates

In 1941 I walked into the Air Ministry and asked with great scepticism if they could use a writer and was staggered and delighted to be told Yes. The Air Ministry of those days went one further, and said they could use a short-story writer. I was accordingly commissioned, given my training in the regulation way, and have never been quite the same man since. I was in fact the first state short-story writer, if that isn't too pompous a name, and my job for the better part of two years was to live with and write about the crews of the RAF. In these two years I wrote enough stories to fill two volumes, each of which subsequently sold, in English alone, something like a quarter of a million copies. From the proceeds of these works, both serially and in volume form, I got nothing in the shape of fees or royalties and of course did not expect anything. The fact that I had written books which sold a quarter of a million copies did not give me financial privileges over and above the men who fought in the air and were paid like me on the basis of rank and not on a commission basis of how many bombs they dropped or how many aircraft they shot down. Taking the pay of a junior commissioned officer at about £400 or £500 a year, it is easy to see that the Treasury in my case was well rewarded. But I too was well rewarded, if not financially; for a writer's dividends are not only in cash, but in the privilege of experience and in what the experience, whatever it is, finally does to him. For my part I found the exhilaration of living with men of action was something that could not and never can be assessed in material terms.

TRAVELLING FOR MAUGHAM

Michael Frayn and Angela Carter are among the winners of the Somerset Maugham Award, a travel grant for under thirty-fives administered by the Society of Authors. *The Author* published these brief reports on their experiences in 1967 and 1970 respectively.

We are all travellers, though many of us will never see with any but the mind's eye; until recently my own journeys were of this kind, borrowing their colour from other people's books and pictures. Now that for me the names of Paris, Bordeaux, Genoa, Florence, Venice, have bulk and presence, can each fall into perspective, it is the mind's eye which views them again. But memory is as different from imagination as the earth from vapours. The experience of travel has given me far more than local colours and faithful atmosphere, far more than the equipment to recreate distant places in words. The gain is incalculable and it is lasting; it will give root and rise to conceptions which could never sprout from any fancy. . . . My experience has become part of the furniture of my mind and will remain, both as an influence and the source of them, long after the details of travel have blurred.

A.L. Barker, winner of the first Maugham Award, Spring 1949

Michael Frayn

I WONDERED ANXIOUSLY from time to time, as I shot round to the supermarket in Stonington, Conn., for another packet of paper nappies, or walked round Phoenix, Ariz., trying to locate the centre of town, exactly what Maugham had in mind when he set up his annual awards for young writers. You have to promise to stay outside the British Isles for at least three months, 'with the object of acquainting yourself with the manners and customs of foreign nations and thereby having an opportunity to increase your experience and knowledge for your future literary benefit'.

I suspect Maugham visualized his young writers as bachelors, able to stay up to all hours and have such affairs as seemed necessary to get the feel of a country's manners and customs properly. One sees the ideal Maugham awardsman sitting at a café table in Singapore, his boater tipped slightly over one eye, watching the passing scene. He meets an older woman of cosmopolitan background who tells him with charming frankness about her varied sexual adventures. He writes up his notes of the conversation as soon as he gets a chance, fanning himself between whiles with his boater, a wry expression on his face. Eventually, in an ornate, slightly peeling hotel bedroom, the lady charmingly seduces him; and he learns a bitter worldly wisdom when he detects her attempting to steal his Award money in the middle of the night . . . .

It would be a logical way for the diligent young writer to

go about the assignment; one's impressions of the countries one visited when one was an even younger writer were greatly coloured by the girls one pursued there, however vainly. It's a rather different experience of foreign nations that one gets, settling into a rented house with one's family. Charming adventuresses come into the picture scarcely at all.

For a start, one patronizes a rather different class of café; the sort where they have the special Little Tommy Tucker menu for children – the sort where they more or less expect to see the milk knocked over. (In one busy midtown restaurant in New York, at the height of the midday rush, each of our two children in turn solemnly knocked over its pint of milk. Had I had a boater, I should have tilted it rakishly right over both eyes.) One gets fairly easily into conversation with charming unadventuresses at nearby tables. 'Oh, bless their little hearts!' they cry. One notes it down, looking as wry as one can, on the back of the Little Tommy Tucker menu.

Margaret Drabble, in Paris on some similar award, reported that seeing the city through the eyes of her children she had come to have a close acquaintance with the varieties of rubbish found on the pavement. Our children, gazing upwards, opened another new world to us – the world of the underside of American luncheon counters; they are all coated with a varicoloured impasto of dried chewing-gum.

'I just love kids!' said an old man in a drugstore to my wife as soon as he saw ours. 'I cut my only son out of my will this morning.'

Even if they keep the adventuresses away, children have their uses as ground bait for some of the other literary material around. It was the children who first attracted the attention of Ouida, for instance. She was sitting in front of us with her husband one afternoon on the Boston–New York train. She leaned round the end of the seat to croodle over the children – a large, soft, croodling woman, dripping with turquoise accessories. Finding that it was uncomfortable to talk to us round the end of the seat, she stood up and addressed us (and all the other passengers in earshot) from the gangway down the middle of the carriage. 'Hey, Colonel,' she called to the conductor, 'will you put me off at Providence? Once I get talking I'm liable to talk myself right past it.'

She was called Ouida, she explained, because her father, a Methodist minister, wanted something a little *risqué*. Her father and her first husband had both been in *Who's Who* – and that was something you couldn't buy for eight bucks a week.

'We've been up in Boston for the weekend,' she told us, and any other young writers who happened to be aboard the train, 'visiting with my granddaughter. I have a granddaughter of twenty-one! She's expecting the stork. Or she thinks she is – they believe it may be a hysterical pregnancy. Listen, we've spent 130 bucks in the last two days! We've poured 130 bucks into the ground! Because they don't appreciate it, you know, they really don't.

'Now, my grandson's a composer. He has the receding hairline of genius! You know what he composes? Electronic music! Have you ever heard any electronic music? Well, either you like it or you don't! Bing – bing – BOING!

'No, it's very good. He really does express the sort of person he is in it, and we're all very proud of him. He's been promised a job teaching music – he'll make fifteen thousand a year.'

The idea that she might talk herself right past Providence kept troubling her, and she took off her watch and gave it to her husband as timekeeper. He was a hotel engineer, she said, at the second most exclusive hotel in New York after the Waldorf. 'They have a room there that costs eighty dollars a day! Imagine: sunken living room – gold taps! And if the gold taps need fixing, it's Johnny that fixes them.

'Johnny doesn't like to talk. He's shy. Hey, stand up, Johnny, and let them take a look at you! Come on!'

A distinguished head, with white hair and black eyebrows, rose above the back of the seat, and smiled silently.

'Johnny's family come from Naples,' said Ouida. 'Do you think he looks Italian? You know what Italians look like – greaseballs! Johnny can't read, but he's very cultured – *really* cultured. All right, you can sit down again now, Johnny.'

The shy smile and white hair disappeared again below the back of the seat.

'Oh, we're just plain folks!' said Ouida. 'Poor but happy! My first husband was rich, and we didn't get along. I often used to go to Johnny's hotel for drinks with my first husband. I never guessed that one day I'd marry the engineer! But you never can tell, can you? You never can tell.'

One sees one's short story, of course. It's set in the second most exclusive hotel in New York. . . . Or more likely: the Boston–New York train, on a close afternoon in early fall. Diligent young English writer, with family. A large, soft woman in the seat in front turns round to tweedle over the children. Her name is Ouida, she announces. . . .

I'll get some literary benefit out of it somehow.

Angela Carter

WHAT DID I DO with my Maugham award? Well, in the end I found I had gone round the world, which surprised me a little; I became a connoisseur of cities, of American, Asiatic and even European cities and encountered, amongst others, the most beautiful transvestite in the whole of Greenwich Village; a Russian wrestler who had a wallet of photographs showing himself wrestling with a bear; a frayed Japanese with nicotine-stained teeth who told me Dostoevsky was his spiritual father; a six-foot-tall girl from Reading striding about Tokyo in a Victorian velvet mantle who modelled for sake ads on Japanese television; hippies, GIs fresh from Vietnam, an ex-para who had jumped into Algeria – and innumerable others.

In America, I saw a great many hallucinatory midnight bus stations and lived in a log cabin in a redwood forest for a while. I heard the windbells of San Francisco and the picturesque cries of the street traders of the Haight-Ashbury quarter (. . . 'hash . . . lids . . . grass . . . '). I made a sentimental journey to the jazz museum in New Orleans and looked at a glass case containing Bix Beiderbecke's collar studs and handkerchief through a mist of tears. Around the Berkeley campus of UCLA, saffron-robed figures sang and danced 'Hare Krishna', to my exquisite embarrassment, and everywhere they advertised burgers – hamburgers, bullburgers, broilerburgers, every kind of burger including Murphy's Irish Shamrockburger. Then I left America and went to

Japan, where people smile and smile but never show their teeth.

Tokyo blazes at night like a neon version of the collected works of Marshall McLuhan and the taxi-drivers wear white gloves. The autumn umbrellas and the willow trees in the streets give this ugliest and most enchanting of cities the atmosphere of a painting by Renoir. At night, beside the vast departmental stores, the fortune-tellers sit at their little stands, each advertised by a neon hand marked with the lines of power, and do a roaring trade. Japan is utterly different from anywhere else in the world. I thought, at first, 'Well, maybe this is just Asia,' but then I went to other Asiatic places and, no, nowhere is the same as Tokyo. And this country, which voluntarily exiled itself from the world for 250 years, is like no other country. I can't say whether I liked it or not, really; only that I was never, even for one moment, bored there.

The Japanese language itself poses – or, rather, annihilates – many problems for the European. For example, there is no Japanese word which roughly corresponds to the great contemporary European supernotion, 'identity'; and there is hardly an adequate equivalent for the verb 'to be'. Further, in a language without plurals, the time-honoured European intellectual division between the one and the many cannot exist except in a kind of intuitive meta-language, the existence of which I very much doubt. Now that I am trying to learn Japanese, I find myself having to turn my head inside out – always good therapy. Japan is like going through the looking-glass and finding out what kind of milk it is that looking-glass cats drink; the same, but totally other. In the campus at Waseda University, beautiful young men with the faces of those who will die on the barricades were lobbing hand grenades at policemen. However, I also went to several other countries.

I travelled, therefore, a great deal, especially for someone who had, previously, never been further than Dublin, Eire, and I saw a great many things: a devil dance who was, I think, bewitching a luxury hotel in Bangkok, which is an unholy blend of Edmund Dulac's illustrations to the *Arabian Nights* and Crawley New Town; sunset over Hong Kong harbour, the waters of which are impossibly green; and finally felt a hunger for the familiar and went to Paris for, though I had never visited there before, I had read about it in Balzac and seen it often in my favourite movie (which is Marcel Carné's *Les Enfants du Paradis*). And it was better than I would have believed possible, and so was the Midi, although the mistral was snarling. In a café in Arles, I saw a madman remove the battered top hat he wore on his head, take from this receptacle the raw chicken which it contained, and eat it.

After that, I came home and tried to sort out, a little, the effects of the enormous barrage of imagery to which I had been subjected and found the task, as these somewhat disconnected paragraphs will indicate, exceedingly difficult. However, I am working on it.

THE MAKING OF
A NOVEL

Under the title of 'Saying Goodbye to Elizabeth',
William Trevor's article opened a series on
'Writers at Work' in Autumn 1973.

The Novel Writers . . . are the great instructors of the country. They help the Church and are better than the Law. They teach ladies to be women, and they teach men to be gentlemen.

Anthony Trollope, speaking at a Royal Literary Fund dinner (quoted in 'On the Side', Summer 1983)

Shirley Conran is reported to have made a million pounds with her first novel, *Lace*, before a single copy was sold. In *The Sunday Times* (22 August) she described how she set out to achieve this success. 'I was determined to reach the American bestseller list. I didn't need to be top, but I had to be in it. And I thought, what's the thing that will do it this year, and I said, "Incest." I decided to try it with one book, and if that wasn't going to make money, I'd stop. I mean, I didn't know if I could write a novel at all.'

Quoted in 'On the Side', Winter 1982

SAYING GOODBYE TO ELIZABETH

William Trevor

'Why', someone said to me, 'do you always dedicate your novels to your wife?' And I said it was because it's my wife, more than my children or my friends, who has to put up with it all.

In 1970 I began the novel I've just corrected the proofs of. I began to write things down on scraps of paper, which I would then lose. Walking about London or Devon, I would think about Elizabeth Aidallbery's daughter, Joanna. She was a nameless child then, just as Elizabeth was, and as Sylvie Clapper and Henry were. Miss Samson didn't even exist, nor did Lily Drucker.

In 1971 it occurred to me that Elizabeth Aidallbery should spend some weeks in hospital, having a hysterectomy. The identity of her ex-husband became clearer, and the part played by Henry in her life became clearer, also. I then abandoned scraps of paper and wrote this:

'On the morning of her admission to hospital Elizabeth was reflected in her mahogany-framed looking-glass while she packed: a thin woman in a grey flannel dress. Outside the house, in cool February sunshine, her daughters waited for her: Jennifer eleven and Alice eight, Joanna seventeen The man who'd been her husband was asleep in Aberdeen, where he now lived. The man who'd briefly been her lover, whose presence in her life had upset her marriage, was reading the magazine section of *The Sunday Times* in a house less than a mile away. In Meridian Close, not far away

223

either, her childhood companion, Henry, shaved himself. In a home for the aged, the Sunset Home in Richmond, her mother ate toast and grapefruit marmalade.'

It's not the first paragraph of the novel, but at the time I assumed it would be. Much later on I wrote the paragraph that is now at the beginning of chapter 1, deciding to start the whole thing off like this: 'At forty-one, Elizabeth Aidallbery had a way of dwelling on her past and when memories were doubtful there were photographs to help her. At two she was anonymous on a tartan rug. At five she was freckled, thin-legged and laughing in a striped dress. At ten she was sun-burnt beneath a tree, her pale hair in plaits, standing with Henry in the garden where her own children played now. There was a wedding photograph, an image that revealed the faded blueness of her eyes because it was in colour.'

I worked spasmodically on this novel, pushing it aside to do other writing, destroying large parts of it, including a good-hearted woman called Frances. In the autumn of 1972 I went to Persia, and dragged Elizabeth Aidallbery and the rest of them with me. By the end of that year I had assembled large quantities of material and had permitted the existence of Lily Drucker's mother-in-law, Dr D'arcy and Dr Carstairs, a public house called The King of England, and Mr Maloney. After a jolly Christmas I sat down to write the thing in earnest. It would be finished, I told my publishers, on 31 May.

Those final five months are no joke for anyone, wives particularly. During the course of completing *Elizabeth Alone*, which was what it had now become, I developed a range of psychosomatic complaints. I was also particularly bad company, refusing to go to dinner with people, and rejecting the joys of alcohol because they interfered with concentration. I had several vivid dreams about Joanna Aidallbery's boyfriend, Samuel; I talked about Miss Samson in my sleep. I convinced myself that if Lily Drucker did have her baby I would have sympathetic labour pains.

I live in Devon and work in a small room overlooking a valley. This room was now entirely devoted to Elizabeth and the others. When the telephone rang the voice that came from it didn't sound like a real voice. I was becoming fonder and fonder of the four women who met when Elizabeth went to have her hysterectomy. But this involvement is not at all another way of saying that fictional characters run away from you and have lives of their own. The idea that people you invent can take off in a direction you don't push them towards has always seemed to me to be specious. As a novelist, you can't afford to permit such fantastic high jinks.

I finished the book at the end of May, working twelve and fourteen hours a day getting it into the shape I wanted. I was haunted by the four women then: Elizabeth herself, tiny Lily Drucker, Sylvie in love with what Sister O'Keefe called Bad News, Miss Samson and the world she'd temporarily left behind her, at 9 Balaclava Avenue. And of course there was the hospital itself, and the autobiography of Lady Augusta Haptree, who'd founded it in 1841 for the women of London's less prosperous classes.

'I determined', Lady Augusta had written, 'that women who were treated no better than water-rats should in sickness at least be offered the privileges of common humanity. There were brought before my husband two men from the Shoreditch neighbourhood who had beaten with chair-legs the wife of one of them because she would not sell the clothes her mother had left her. In the hospital to which this woman was brought nothing was done for her. Nurses refused to undress her, believing her to be a street-walker. She was unable to undress herself and died on the third day of her confinement, the wounds beneath her clothes having taken in poison. That the hospital should bear a share of guilt equal to that for which the two men were imprisoned I have no doubt. Yet a hospital can be judged only by the law of God.'

Lady Augusta died in 1901. On 29 April I walked into a

room and for a split second imagined that she was sitting on a sofa.

I had a reluctance to part with the novel, but it was slipping from me anyway. It was all so neat now, nicely typed, and read by the typist and by my wife. Before that, no one but I had known even the name of a single character. On 4 June I handed the typescript over to my publishers and was aware of a sense of desolation and bereavement. I didn't want to say goodbye to Elizabeth and the others, or to Mr Alstrop-Smith, the gynaecologist with total recall, or even to Mr Maloney and the ageing hippy, Mrs Tabor-Ellis. For such a long time now they'd been my own private people, imaginary friends who did what they were told.

But it wasn't really until I'd corrected the proofs of this book that I felt the real unhappiness of parting. A love affair of a kind had ended and only technicalities were left: the green ink of the printer's correcting ballpoint pen, my own blue-black. Depression settled on me, and posting off the proofs was like lowering a coffin. I would never again be involved with these people.

For me, only novels are like this. Plays work in the opposite way: until the people in them are shared with actors and actresses they're not really human documents. And the time spent writing a short story is too brief to permit the conjuring up of relationships with its characters. But the novels cause havoc enough, and what the wife to whom I dedicate them has to put up with is a querulous customer who's always about the place, who performs work about which he won't talk, who mutters in his sleep about imaginary women, who longs to get the thing finished and then enters a depression because he has to post a set of proofs. And the unfortunate fact is that it gets worse with every novel. Saying goodbye to Elizabeth was the most mournful farewell of all.

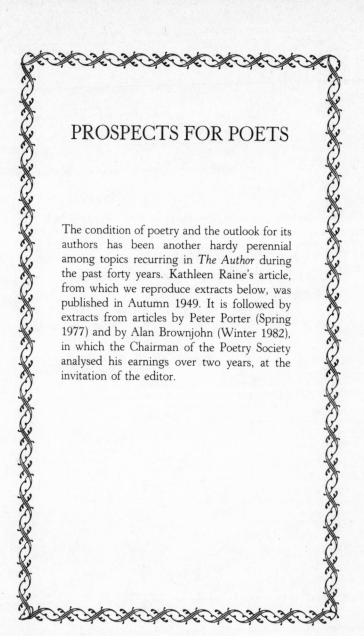

PROSPECTS FOR POETS

The condition of poetry and the outlook for its authors has been another hardy perennial among topics recurring in *The Author* during the past forty years. Kathleen Raine's article, from which we reproduce extracts below, was published in Autumn 1949. It is followed by extracts from articles by Peter Porter (Spring 1977) and by Alan Brownjohn (Winter 1982), in which the Chairman of the Poetry Society analysed his earnings over two years, at the invitation of the editor.

On the whole, it is a flat time, and publishers have nothing to say to poets, regarding them as unprofitable people. Quite; but the fact that the sentence I have just written comes from the autobiography of Sir Henry Taylor (1800–1886), and refers to the 1830s, may usefully remind us that this lamentable situation is no new misfortune.

Janet Adam Smith, 'The Poet's Lot',
Winter 1954

HOW ARE POETS TO LIVE?

Kathleen Raine

THE FINANCIAL difficulties of poets are of a special kind; less demoralizing, perhaps, than those of novelists, who must always cherish a secret hope that a book will earn for them a substantial sum of money, and whose impatience with poverty must be correspondingly heightened by this hope. Poets, who know very well that no amount of fame will bring them a fortune, are at least spared this uncertainty. We know that we cannot expect to earn even a substantial part of our living expenses by writing verse. During the war, conditions for poetry were exceptionally good. My own first volume went quickly into a second edition, and I believe that between four and five thousand copies were sold. My second volume, published in 1946, has barely sold out an edition of two thousand, and I am told that the sales of many poets whose names are fairly well known are at present even lower, a matter not of thousands but of hundreds of copies. I mention my own experience because I am, I imagine, an average poet in this respect. But it is certain that not even Auden, or Dylan Thomas (who has more recently become very widely known), probably not T.S. Eliot himself, could hope to live on the proceeds of their verse, even in the most modest way – and poets, heaven knows, seldom like, or need, to live expensively.

The poems published in volumes of verse have, of course, as a rule been published in periodicals beforehand, and sometimes in anthologies, and in America, and elsewhere.

But many poetry periodicals have no money themselves, and every poet, I fancy, gives away a fair number of poems every year.

The rates paid by newspapers like the *New Statesman*, the *Listener*, *Time and Tide* and *Tribune* vary between 10s 6d to three or four guineas for a short poem. *Horizon* pays two guineas for a sonnet, and up to five guineas for a poem that runs over the page – and these are the highest rates, paid to the best poets in the country. The rates paid by the BBC for poems broadcast are a little higher; but no poet can expect to have his work broadcast very often – two or three single poems in a year perhaps. As for a broadcast programme of a poet's work, one may have to wait a lifetime for that. I myself have been asked to do a number of things for the BBC (including writing poems to commission), but a programme of my work has never been broadcast. I do not say this as having a strong sense of grievance, but only to indicate that it is a fairly unusual thing for poets to have programmes of their work broadcast. When one considers, besides, that scarcely any of the weekly or monthly reviews publish more than one or two poems in an issue, it is very clear that no single poet can possibly publish enough poems in a year to make any appreciable income. Most newspapers regard poems as useful fill-ups for columns. It is only in *Horizon*, the late *Poetry London*, and a few other papers, that long poems are published at all. Who has ever heard of one of the weeklies devoting a whole page to poetry? The only exception I recall is a weekly that few people have heard of that published Eliot's *Four Quartets*.

These facts are likely to be overlooked by the world at large, because, in some strange way, the prestige of poets is high in spite of everything – higher, I fancy, than that of novelists. The international fame of T.S. Eliot, and the considerable status of poets like Edith Sitwell and Auden and Spender may well be misleading to the public who would do wrong to imagine that the income derived by these poets from their work bears any relation to their celebrity. In this respect, the position of poets is very much worse than that of painters. It may be many years before a painter finds recognition, but when he does, he can perfectly well live by his painting without compromising his standards as an artist. A drawing sold for ten or twenty guineas is equivalent, in work and inspiration, to a poem for which a poet will receive two or three from a periodical. An exhibition of paintings may well represent a thousand pounds to a fairly well-known painter, while a poet, for a volume of verse that has occupied him for about the same time as a painter takes to prepare a London exhibition, is not very likely to receive more than a hundred pounds in royalties at the present time.

How, then, are poets to live? Obviously by some other form of employment, or some form of patronage, unless, as happens rarely in these days, they have private means. On the face of it, there seems no reason why poets should not take some sort of job, and write verse in their spare time. The writing of poetry does not require a special light, as does painting, or hours of practice, like music. But a pencil, a sixpenny notebook, and inspiration are not, for all that, all that a poet needs. Poetry is an art that must be practised. It has a language and a rhetoric that must be studied.

A poet must have time to read as well as to think and feel; most poets nowadays suffer from lack of time for reading, and much verse is fragmentary and amateur in consequence. A poet who works as a motor mechanic (as did one whose name is little short of famous), or as a bank clerk, like one of the most talented of the not so young younger poets, cannot give enough time to the study of a technique that is no less highly specialized than that of music and painting, although (like painting in this respect also) its effect may be simple.

But why should not a poet take a job as a university don, or a schoolmaster, or in the BBC, or the British Council, at some work not wholly unconnected with poetry? Some poets can and do make some compromise, but others – and some of the best – are unemployable. They are good for nothing but writing poetry. To be employable for a poet is often a misfortune so far as his poetry is concerned. A man cannot serve two masters, and routine of any kind, any prescribed duty, is the enemy of inspiration, of the habit of attending to that inner voice. In practice, besides, the jobs that the modern world offers nearly all demand many hours a day of our time; and all our physical and nervous strength – much more so than similar jobs in the nineteenth century, as Virginia Woolf has said. They also demand a kind of interest and loyalty, a belief in the thing being done, that a poet either cannot give, or that insidiously saps his genius. No one will deny that a teacher or a doctor (I know poets who are, or have been, both) should give his heart, as well as his time, to his work. And to be a teacher or a doctor nowadays is an exacting employment. The expense of spirit in the wastes of bureaucracy I will pass over; nor is the mercurial existence of journalism right for poets. This profession has changed little since Balzac wrote *Les Illusions perdues*; there is still the endless round of seeing people, selling one's talent and one's time, reading and reviewing ephemeral books and plays that give the mind little sustenance in return for hours wasted in producing articles forgotten as soon as read.

Poets, like other men, need to move among those engaged in the same kind of work, the same kind of thought. To take a job is often, in the modern world, to go into exile, to be among men, whether bankers or mechanics or cultural bureaucrats, whose interests and skill are of a different kind. The writing of poetry is a serious occupation that requires thought and skill, and it is vain to imagine that great verse can be written in spare hours, while the poet's workmates are filling in football pools or going to the dog races – or, to be less bitter, growing vegetables or listening to the Third Programme. One may write a few lyrics in that way, but not

232

The Faerie Queene or *Paradise Lost* or *The Prelude* or Pound's *Cantos*. And all too few poets nowadays are in a position even to consider a long work on that scale. In practice, nearly all jobs today are more than full time, and very exhausting. Is it reasonable to expect the poet to begin his real work when his fellow workers stop theirs?

It may be salutary for a poet to go through some such *saison en enfer* – but as a permanent solution it is unthinkable.

As poets go, I myself am – or was, reasonably employable. But I regret no years so much as the few that I spent in a government department, and a cultural organization. They yielded me nothing but a salary, and made me a worse poet and a worse person. I have since compromised with the world in a way that allows me freedom of mind, and time, in exchange for a good deal of worry. Like many poets, I can earn just enough money by translating (not well-paid work either), book reviewing, a little broadcasting and lecturing and critical writing, to live in a very modest way indeed, and with an ever-present spectre at my elbow, never knowing how I shall be able to pay the next bill. To live in this way – and many poets do – requires a great deal of faith in the miraculous; a faith, by the way, that is usually justified, for the human spirit is, finally, stronger than the material powers of the world. But often the cost to the nerves is one that no one, not even a poet, can afford to go on paying year after year, without damage to his physical health, or his talent, or both. And there is always the danger that the anxiety of this precarious freedom will dry up the springs of poetry just as surely as the perpetual distractions of journalism, the fatuities of bureaucracy, or the fatigue of physical toil. I can speak from bitter personal experience of the difficulty that I suppose nearly all poets have to encounter, of sailing between the Scylla of losing one's soul and strength in a job other than one's vocation, and the Charybdis of a too anxious freedom. This situation exists, you understand, because it is not in the nature of our present society

233

possible for poets to earn enough money, as other men do, or should be able to do, by devoting themselves to the work that is their true work in the world – work as necessary as tilling the soil or teaching the young, if civilization means anything at all.

What is the solution? A congenial part-time job is hard to find, but not impossible. With all deference to Dr Johnson, patronage, I believe, is the best of all. Joyce, Yeats and Rilke had no hesitation in accepting help from patrons, and rightly so, knowing full well that they were repaying the world in coinage more precious than gold. The very greatest artists will never refuse the help of patrons, because they know the value of their work. Unfortunately there is always a worthless fringe to the literary world who will accept money from less honourable motives – plausible and assertive characters who have more talent for securing money than for writing. Between the giants who are above personal pride, and the parasites who are beneath it, there is a considerable body of writers of talent, many of whom will suffer great hardship rather than ask for help, or even accept it; and it is these who create the climate of the literary world out of which great works grow.

And many poets would have time to starve ten times over before reaching the eminence that places the great ones above the pressure of necessity that kills talent in the early stages. In the matter of discrimination, the private patron, who takes a human risk and human responsibility, as well as a financial one, is less likely to go wrong, I believe, and more likely to discover great talent in its early stages, than any public body. The next best are publishers, who have a profit motive, but who are not under political or popular control, who are, besides, capable of disinterestedness, and likely to get to know writers of talent and their work in the course of their profession. Public bodies would be likely, as I see it, to give money neither to the best nor the worst, but to the respectable general run of mediocre poets and artists, whose work is comprehensible at a first reading and likely to offend no one. I doubt whether any state fund in Europe would have given a farthing to the author of *Ulysses* – in fact, they all banned his books. But whatever the drawbacks of public as compared with private patronage, it is the only possible solution in a socialist state, and better than nothing at all.

There are, besides, the universities. It seems to me likely that both the universities and the poets would benefit if every university were to follow the example to be set, I understand, by one of them, of making a grant to at least one creative writer, who would be resident, or in a loose way attached, to the university.

So the English faculties might be given a liveliness that they do not always possess, by the proximity of living genius; and poets, who need, or ought to need, libraries and the society of intelligent minds in their own and other spheres, would benefit no less. Apart from this special patronage, the leisure and freedom still enjoyed in a measure by university dons would make this one of the professions that poets could follow as an avocation without too much strain, but not all poets are qualified to do so.

The poet needs one thing above all – the sense of freedom, and the knowledge that his bare existence, at all events, will remain secure. A lump sum earned or given, that assures us of three or six months' security, is not enough, if at the end the prospect is no better than at the beginning. Unless some better way is found of enabling poets to live in our present form of society, there will cease to be poets. 'That fine delight that fathers thought' does not come to the desperately worried, or to those who have sold themselves as day labourers to work, however honourable and valuable in itself, that is not their true vocation.

FREELANCING WITH POETRY

Peter Porter

I CAME TO LONDON [from Australia] in 1951 and for the next eight years worked as a clerk or in bookselling. I belonged to that generation which thought that the way to become a writer was to support oneself by working during the day and to compose one's poems, plays or novels at night or over the weekend. Our generation was not attracted by academic life, and there were no grants and handouts. We believed that you wrote your works and sent them to editors and that one day, when you wrote well enough, you would be published. What happened then, as young girls used to feel about marriage, was delicious but rather hazy. Once you were published, all sorts of good things would occur. The truth, alas, is rather different. Once you are published as a poet, you may have the chance to become a critic or an arts journalist, but if you do, you will live a life of deadlines and commissions, with only luck or heroism to keep your own poetry writing going. But the most important quality in a poet is persistence, and those who give up, however talented they may have been initially, cannot call themselves poets.

I was working in advertising when my first book was published [in 1961]. In the nine years I stayed in advertising I increased my yearly quota of occasional journalism steadily. I began to pay two different kinds of tax – PAYE through my employers and schedule D on my freelance earnings. But in the year when I quit advertising for good (1968 – and I have never done one word of copywriting since), I was making less than £1,000 as a freelance. Advertising attracts the attention of the Juvenals and Origens of our day, as well as of the comic novelists and myth-makers. In my time, it was not a very well-paid profession, though it had several advantages for the writer. The hours were flexible and one's employers were understanding up to a point. So half the poems which appear in my second and third books were composed 'in the boss's time'. I am grateful to my several superiors for this, as much as for the money they paid me. But the ice age was coming, and when the small American-based agency to which I had gone in 1968 decided to offer me an asbestos handshake (about £600, and more than my goodwill was worth, I suspect) I took it.

Thus I found myself facing the world as a freelance writer in September 1968. My wife supported me totally in my decision never to take a regular office job again. My children, of course, were not asked their opinion. It was now that the work I had done over the previous five or six years stood me in good stead. I was offered reviewing opportunities in journals and, especially, on the radio. It would be quite improper for me to conjecture on my effectiveness in either medium, but I can say, with certainty, that I am forever indebted to many friends in professional places who had confidence in me and gave me plenty of work. At the same time, I must stress that this was not nepotism – *that* will get you a job only once. Nor an old-boy net – I am not even redbrick or white-tile, let alone Oxbridge. It's worth insisting on the openness of the literary market here, since so many people continue to believe in metropolitan conspiracies and the like. From what I have seen of America and Australia, I have no hesitation in declaring that England is the most open of all societies.to the man of talent. If it were not, there would be no gossip of 'an Australian Mafia', and the rest. (If there is one, I do not belong to it.)

I saw very clearly, from the beginning of my life as a full-time freelance, that my main danger was in letting my poetry lapse, as deadline followed deadline, and offers I couldn't refuse were made to me. In fact, this never happened, for which I must thank my lazy nature. No matter how pressing a review might be, I could always drop it for a poem. Writing poetry is the only form of literary labour which gives me entire satisfaction. This doesn't mean it is easy or that the results are worth the effort – merely that the sense of relief at a tension's being relaxed is enormous, when you have been obsessed by a notion for a poem. And, curiously, your reviewing can act as a catalyst. This is something which serious poets don't like to admit. A book sent for review, one which you might never have dreamed of looking at in the ordinary course of reading, can lead to an original poem, and often a good one. This, I call 'saving from the wreck' – and the life of every freelance is a daily swim out to his shattered expectations to bring ashore both the comforts and the achievements of his life. . . .

Previous contributors to this series have been much more forthcoming about sums of money and daily expenses than I have. I am not being cagey to mislead the Inland Revenue, but I have small taste for figures spread over a page. At present, I make about £4,000 a year directly from freelancing. It is hardly a liveable income in London. (Some eyebrows may be raised in the stormy fens and elsewhere at this remark.) I could step it up to almost £6,000 if I worked like a donkey. More important to me (and I do not own any property or even a car – just some books and records) is the fact that I am still writing poetry. I should like to write better, but to achieve that I shall have to go on earning my keep. My dream would be to write music – something I cannot do. But I can still compose poems, and I am glad that my way of life permits me to.

LIVING ON POETRY

Alan Brownjohn

SINCE THESE REFLECTIONS on what I earn from writing are going to sound several notes of complaint and bewilderment, I ought to start by putting on record one advantage I enjoy in company with a few others. In the late 1970s I was made redundant from my permanent lecturing post in teacher training; a consequence of the wholesale contraction in this area of higher education which followed Mrs Thatcher's White Paper *A Framework for Expansion* (1972). . . . Three years later, after strenuous freelance efforts, the annual compensation still constitutes almost half of my total income, which is still less than what I earned as a lecturer.

Every active freelance must wonder whether he or she *might* be able to maximize earnings with superhuman work loads, letting no offer or opportunity pass. ('Might' may come to seem an increasingly appropriate word: there are likely to be more and more of us coming into the small literary freelance market from education.) The genuinely agonizing question is whether you sacrifice personal writing time to earn what you need from ancillary literary activities. The dilemma is simple and very harsh: Do I clear my diary and write, knowing what derisory rewards accrue from such dedication? Or do I go and search for the modest income to be derived from the literary jobbing, somehow just hoping that there will still be time for the writing? Can I *afford* to do what I *should* be doing?

Mostly, I would surmise, writers take day-to-day decisions

239

on this dilemma, not often working out the detailed arith-
metic of their literary earnings and considering the implications (at least, I know few poets who do: their literary
lives, more than most others, are a labyrinth of small-scale
literary activities). I have recently tried – laboriously, but the
exercise fascinates and alarms – to do some of these calcu-
lations; and I find they produce disconcerting answers. It
will require a personal table; something crudely compiled *by*
a non-statistician *for* non-statisticians, but I hope it provides
a fairly accurate basis for some conclusions to be drawn.

In percentage terms, in the financial years 1980–81 and
1981–82, one poet's literary earnings looked like this:

		1980–81	1981–82
1	Radio work	35.5	25.6
2	Poetry readings in schools	18.5	15.5
3	Creative writing courses and workshops	16.7	19.1
4	Reviewing and occasional journalism	7.9	8.3
5	Public poetry readings	6.9	14.5
6	Royalties, permission fees	6.9	2.3
7	Fees for new poems published in journals, anthologies, broadcast, etc.	2.5	3.3
8	Judging competitions	0.3	4.6
9	Other	4.8	6.8
		100.0	100.0

The categories may need a little explanation. 'Radio' (1)
comprises all kinds of broadcasting work other than new
poems newly broadcast, including the compiling and presenting of poetry programmes, features for schools radio,
permission fees for 'old' poems broadcast in series on Radios
3 and 4. Schools poetry readings (2) are just that: you go in,
read, and answer questions; which is quite different from a

creative writing workshop, or residential course, conducted with either children or adults (3). Public poetry readings (5) are given to the general public, attending (unlike some school pupils) quite voluntarily the readings and festivals staged by hard-working arts organizers up and down the country. Royalties and permission fees (6) are earned by books; fees for new poems (7) are earned by publication in magazines, new verse anthologies, radio poetry programmes and the like. Will PLR appear on the list in 1984–85, I wonder . . .?

The small variations between the two years are not indicative of any trends (the trends were well established before 1980: I shall come back to them). Rather they represent matters of chance, and not the energetic cultivation of any particular plot. Thus, radio commissions had a good year in 1980–81. Public poetry readings earned more in 1981–82 purely because of a substantial fee for one week's heavy touring. In the latter year I yielded more often to the plea to judge poetry competitions than I really like to. In 1980–81 I published what was, for me, a slow writer, a largish collection of poems, my first for five years, which was tolerably well received and chosen for distribution to the members of the Poetry Book Society. It helped to raise my royalties from books to the dizzying height of 6.9 per cent. Apart from these shifts, the steady sources of (very modest) income recently remain much the same from year to year. About 80 per cent of this income derives not, to draw a distinction, from 'writing and publishing poetry' but from 'being a poet'. If I tried to live entirely on writing and publishing my verse in magazines and books, and did not (or could not) also give public readings of it, I would have earned precisely £810 in the whole two years in question.

To expound this from my table of statistics: in 1980–81, personal creativity produced, under items (6) and (7), precisely 9.4 per cent of earnings, some of that accruing from permission fees for anthology publication of poems written long ago. Add to this fees for public readings of my own work and it makes 16.2 per cent that I think of as earnings from sources which acknowledge my writing for its own sake. (The same sums produce 20.1 per cent for 1981–82.) I ponder about the status of school poetry readings; and I come to the conclusion that their purpose is almost always a (thoroughly worthy) educational one: the schools primarily want you to come and demonstrate that poetry in general is a good and pleasurable thing; they are not primarily honouring your own work. For this reason, I put item (2) in with the rest; the non-creative literary work that arrives as a result of 'being a poet' (a fact which enables you to review, judge, write for radio and, or course, teach poetry writing).

I am sure that this trend towards the 'educational' in the activities of poets is to be welcomed, provided the poets enjoy it and do it well. At the same time, the dependence on it for one third of my own literary income (combining items (2) and (3)) – a proportion which I would *guess* to be an average one for freelance poets – sometimes gives me pause. Invitations to read poems to fourth-formers, or to conduct creative writing workshops with them, are some sort of testimony to the power of poetry as an art. But is all this producing readers? Or is the poet gradually becoming an adjunct to the efforts of English teachers? If that is the case, then the poet should insist on going into schools on his or her own terms, not as someone who fits neatly and unobtrusively into some part of the English Department timetable.

There are, in the multifarious activities which provide a poet's income, many pleasures of which the poet is glad. School visits and public readings, writing courses in remote and attractive places, visits to the broadcasting studios – they all release him (guiltily sometimes) from his typewriter. But I know of hardly any poet who would not like to change the balance represented by those percentages. For one thing, it would not – when one looks at the small number of ways in which they can earn cash by writing – take many small disasters to wipe out poets' main sources of income overnight. Radio broadcasting seems safe enough? The introduction of commercial cable television would cheapen public-service broadcasting and starve it of funds; what chance would poetry on BBC Radio 3 and 4 have in that atmosphere? Purblind monetarism could dry up even the tiny springs of cash which send writers into the schools or out to tutor the courses. Freezing winds of recession could blow down even more of the few magazine outlets for literary journalism and poetry that still exist. But then the situation where poets have become dependent on these 'ancillary' sources for all except a derisory percentage of their earnings should not have developed at all.

It seems to me that any discussion of the low earnings of writers from writing leads back (since literature, luckily in some ways, has never been a glamorous candidate for advertisers' sponsorship) to what might be achieved by even a small increase in public subsidy. The availability in the past of grants to individual writers, and today of grants to publishers for individual books, merely skirts the main issue; which is, that the most basic kind of *institutional* infrastructure for the support of literature does not exist as it does for the other arts, and urgently needs to be created. Part of it could be created by helping (financially, of course) existing organiz-ations to achieve at least some of the status and esteem automatically accorded the major institutions in the other arts. But the one reform most needed would not require showmanship or flair for publicity, only dogged application to a very ordinary, obvious but difficult task. The equivalent for poetry and fiction of major institutions like the National Theatre, the Royal Opera and the Tate is, quite simply, a countrywide distribution scheme which would give scores of thousands of readers – those who bought *Penguin Modern Poets* – the incentive and the opportunity to purchase the literary magazines and, above all, the books.

I would just like my *writing* to bring in a little more than

243

9.4 per cent of a literary income which, in any case, is only just over 50 per cent of what I receive. Without the (unindexed) compensation I receive as one of the privileged white-collar redundant, the crumbs earned from full-time freelance literary work would not keep me at all.

PROS AND CONS
OF EXILE

Punitive taxation in recent years has driven a
handful of writers to weigh the assets against
the drawbacks of temporary emigration; but
the literary exile described in the following
article is of a different kind. It was contributed
to *The Author* in Spring 1977 by Francis King,
then Chairman of the Society's Committee of
Management.

In some far-flung places, small bribes, *baksheesh* or tips to beggars are normal, because local salaries and social services are so meagre. Give willingly, and without moral indignation. One day, if the book you are writing is long and difficult and the place alluring, you may be a beggar yourself.

Jack Beeching, 'Making Out Abroad', Autumn 1972

ABROAD THOUGHTS FROM HOME

Francis King

AT THE CLOSE OF *A Portrait of the Artist as a Young Man,* Stephen Dedalus decides to quit Ireland. To his friend Cranly he explains the reasons for his decision: 'I will not serve that in which I no longer believe, whether it call itself my home, my fatherland, or my church; and I will try to express myself in some mode of life or art as freely as I can and as wholly as I can, using for my defence the only arms that I allow myself to use – silence, exile, and cunning.' Like his hero, Joyce also abandoned Ireland, never to return, keeping his vow of 'Non serviam' so scrupulously that the subsequent struggles of his country to achieve independence left no trace whatsoever in his work. Joyce was not of course the only major twentieth-century writer of the English-speaking world to make this resolve.

A critic has described Joyce's style as 'more cosmopolitan than any in modern literature' and it is this cosmopolitanism that, for good or ill, is usually the first fruit of exile. But by going abroad the British writer may also achieve something as important or even more important: escape from a rigid class structure. So many of the leading novelists of our time – Anthony Powell, Angus Wilson, Henry Green, even Ivy Compton-Burnett – have given close attention to the infinite number of class nuances that in this strange country of ours have somehow obstinately survived the colossal upheavals of two major wars, the communization of half of Europe and a succession of Labour governments. Considerations less parochial have in consequence been ignored.

Class in England also acts as a fence over which the novelist must scramble in order to learn about people higher or lower in the pecking order than himself. When I first began to write, I was terribly conscious of that fence. Perhaps if I had been less shy and more of an extrovert, I should not have felt so embarrassed and clumsy when trying to become familiar with people not of my own kind. My embarrassment and clumsiness no doubt communicated themselves; so that even when, during the war, I was a farm labourer among other farm labourers, I had a sense of remaining irrevocably an outsider, set apart by my 'posh' or 'la-di-da' way of talking.

Going abroad, I still remained different; but now the difference was simply that I was an Englishman among Italians, Greeks, Finns or Japanese. Few foreigners were competent to place me in any class, since the elaborate code book that provides the key to a man's place in the English class structure was not generally available. Conversely, the class structure in, say, Italy, was a mystery to me. There were rich and poor people, there were people with titles and people without them, there were workers on the land and workers in industry or commerce. It was no more clear than that. I was glad of that liberation from the English obsession and I am sure that it did me nothing but good, since it enabled me to concentrate on differences – moral, intellectual, psychological – of far greater moment.

I also found that when, during my fifteen-year period of exile, I used to return to England, I viewed the country not with eyes dulled by familiarity but as a foreigner might. After even a two-year absence I would notice changes that my family and friends had entirely failed to notice, so imperceptibly had they taken place around them. Things that had never struck me as particularly beautiful or note-worthy when I had been resident in England would now impress me deeply. Often I would stop to stare at something that seemed totally ordinary to my companions of the moment; but for me it had ceased to be ordinary, it had become exotic. Similarly I also found myself viewing the people of this country as though they were foreigners; and setting them against the people of the country in which I was resident, I would be aware of comparisons both favourable and unfavourable.

Yet I think that there are also dangers in too prolonged an exile. The first of these is to regard as national traits what are merely traits common to all humanity. How typically Italian, how typically Greek, how typically Finnish, how typically Japanese, I'd find myself exclaiming, when all I really meant was that some action was typically human in its vulgarity, unreliability, dullness, evasiveness or whatever it might be. 'National character' had become almost as dangerous a preoccupation as class once had been for me.

There was also the threat of rootlessness: the cosmopolitan's dilemma of belonging everywhere and nowhere. When a writer adopts a single country, as Henry James, Joseph Conrad and T.S. Eliot adopted England and as W.H. Auden and Christopher Isherwood adopted the United States, or when a writer is concerned not with the present but with the past, as James Joyce was concerned with the Dublin of Bloomsday, then this threat usually exists only in that period of readjustment, immediately after transplantation, when the roots are reaching down for sustenance. But the nature of my career in the British Council was such that every four years or so I had to tear up roots and then start to put them down again somewhere else. I found each new country tremendously stimulating, so that a host of fresh ideas for short stories and novels would at once crowd in on me; but often, I am afraid, what stimulated me were brilliant surfaces, dazzling to the eye, rather than secret depths that I had not yet had time to locate, let alone plumb.

There is also (to be cynical) a practical difficulty for any writer who wishes to make a name for himself in exile. Viewed in the national context, English literary life is unusually metropolitan; viewed in a world context, it is unusually provincial. . . . In this country 'out of sight, out of mind' tends to be the rule for writers unless, like Muriel Spark, Christopher Isherwood or Graham Greene, they have already laid the foundations of their reputations before going abroad. Moreover, in the country of one's adoption people are unlikely to value one as a writer unless they first know that one is valued back at home. (The only exception to this rule is Japan, where foreign writers are flatteringly accepted at their own valuations.)

Exile can be enormously useful to a writer, enabling him, in the words of Stephen Dedalus's mother, 'to learn . . . away from home and friends what the heart is and what it feels'. But if the writer shuttles ceaselessly from one foreign country to another for too long, there is a real danger that the heart will eventually shrivel up and feel nothing at all for lack of sustenance. There have often been moments when, overwhelmed by the frustrations and distractions of life in England, I have, like George Herbert, 'struck the board and cried "No more; I will abroad,"' but I think that, on balance, it has been wiser for me to have resisted that impulse.

CHANGING MEDIA

Looking cautiously ahead in 1911 at 'the importance of cinematography to dramatic authors', the Society's journal acknowledged that while playwrights might soon be making 'a regular income from this form of reproduction', it might also become of great importance to other authors, including 'technical writers in all the various branches of knowledge and science'. From then on *The Author* was frequently concerned with cinematic matters: in 1914, two months after war broke out, a cinema subcommittee of the Society was established and endured until 1937 when the Screenwriters' Association was formed. The problems of writing for radio began to be reflected in *The Author* during the 1920s; and, from the 1950s, those of writing for television.

Authors must get away from the idea that anything is 'good enough for the films'. . . . Write sincerely and plausibly; imagination is good in its proper place, but do not forget that real life contains all the stories necessary.

Michael Balcon, 'Home Truths for Authors III', Spring 1933

The coming of television will certainly mean the beginning of the end of the film industry as we know it. . . . There will be a prolonged struggle between the two forms of reproduction or transmission, which will enter its decisive phase with the establishment of chains of television theatres competing with the screen theatres. It is pleasant to think that authors as well as actors will be disputed between the rival forces, for their rewards ought to increase accordingly.

Ashley Dukes, Winter 1936

FROM FILM TO THEATRE

Roger MacDougall

The article from which we have taken the extracts below was published under the title of 'Dream and Reality' in Summer 1951.

HAVING RECENTLY EMERGED from the dream world of film into the quasi-reality of theatre, I feel that some comparative impressions may be of interest. That the film world is indeed a dream world may be denied by many, indeed by almost all of those who live in it. But it has to be admitted that to the dreamer the dream *is* reality. And only in the waking state can he realize retrospectively that it was hallucinatory. . . .

Let me now come down to earth with a number of categorical statements – which must all be qualified, of course, with an understood 'in my opinion' or 'in my experience'.

1 Playwriting is more lucrative than screenwriting.
2 Playwriting is more satisfying than screenwriting.
3 The playwright has more control over the finished product than the screenwriter.
4 In the theatre, the writer is consulted about producer, cast and settings, as of right. In the studio he is frequently ignored.
5 The writer whose primal interest is a love of words will be lost in the cinema, and will find his soul again when he enters the theatre.

6 The mental age of a theatre audience is several years above that of a cinema audience. It is at least adolescent.

7 In the theatre the actor approaches a part from the assumption that it is his job to do what you have written. In the studio a star approaches his part from the assumption that it is your job to write what he can do.

8 A play is the author's play. For better or worse, he is responsible. A film is first the producer's, second the star's, third the director's, or fourth a combination of these. It is never the author's.

9 A writer for the screen is forced to part with all his rights. In so far as the property has any subsequent value, the advantage belongs to the production company. In the theatre, a play remains the property of the dramatist, and may earn him money for many years after its first London run.

10 Because of the nature of the industry and the large amounts of money involved in its production, a film must always appeal to the majority. In the theatre, despite the hold of commercialism, there is still room for minorities.

At this point I propose to break off from the delightful task of making categorical statements in order to see whether or not they can be substantiated, and whether or not reservations have to be made.

To the *first* statement I would add the reservation that one talks here of a successful playwright. In fairness it must be admitted that the unsuccessful playwright will starve while the unsuccessful screenwriter may well pick up a tolerable income. This rather anomalous state of affairs is due to the fact that there are not usually enough screenwriters to go round, mainly because there are so many producers and directors who take the floor uneasily unless at least six and preferably a dozen writers have been let loose on the subject between conception and final script. In theory the script becomes more and more brilliant as each fresh mind is brought to bear on it. In practice a lowest common denominator factor comes into operation, and the script grows increasingly mediocre. Some day, no doubt, it will be realized that screenwriting is much like other forms of writing – a creative job done best by an artist in solitude, or at most by a collaboration. At the moment it is bedevilled by the mumbo-jumbo of its technique (which is only newer and not more difficult than stage technique) and there we will leave it.

The *second* statement is entirely a matter of personal experience. I can truthfully state that I have never found pleasure in watching a film I have written. Equally truthfully I can affirm that watching a performance of a play is a smugly exciting experience.

Three is, I think, undeniable. A stage producer will not cut a line or alter a phrase except in consultation with the author. I have attended the rehearsals of all my plays. Moreover, both these rights are granted in the normal play contract.

Four is a right similarly provided for in the normal contract in theatre; never, in my experience, in film.

My *fifth* statement is again a matter of personal idiosyncrasy. It is true that both the theatre and the cinema portray action. But in film the visual portrayal is generally more important than the verbal, whereas the reverse is normally true of a play. A film can be likened to a chemical process actually taking place. A play is more deeply concerned with the analysis of the residue than with the observation of the catalysis. There are exceptions in both media, but by and large, a film is a happening while a play can be a reflection. In the first, words have a utilitarian function. In the second, an artistic.

Statement *six* is perhaps a prejudice, but I think it's true on the average.

Seven is, in my experience, incontrovertible. The whole climate of film – for which I'm afraid writers are themselves largely responsible – reduces the writer to the status of a lackey. Star worship in film is much like star worship in the theatre. But the writer has somehow allowed himself to be pushed off the balloon. As a result, he is a comparative nonentity (which doesn't really matter) and wields no very great authority (which matters considerably). He is the servant of the company and thus comes to be regarded as the servant of director and stars, too. In the long run the film industry and the public who pay to see its products are the sufferers. In the interests of these, as well as his own, the writer must fight (a) to be worthy of primary importance in the industry and (b) to see that he gets it.

Statement number *eight* is really a corollary of seven. It is the film writer's job to get on equal terms of recognition with his more fortunate brother, the dramatist. No one else will do it for him. If he succeeds, he will find that a film is reviewed as his, that he is held responsible for its success or failure, that he is adequately publicized as its author, and that press reviews will discuss more or less intelligently what he has tried to do. But he must overcome many deep-rooted habits and prejudices. A position once lost is doubly difficult to regain.

Number *nine* is again a corollary of the lackey status. Again the screenwriter has only himself to blame. Again his salvation is in his own hands.

Ten, however, is out of his hands. It is an occupational hazard. The screenwriter can with justice complain that the IQ of film audiences is underestimated by some producers and all distributors. But he cannot ignore the principle.

I have tried to put down on paper the reflections of a sleeper who has awakened. Those who are still comfortably asleep will doubtless dismiss my reflections as prejudices. In a sense they are. But at least they are prejudices born of experience and not merely of theoretical analysis.

Film could be an exciting medium to explore. But, for the moment at least, the conditions do not encourage exploration. I personally find the world of theatre more exciting, more stimulating, and more rewarding in every sense.

FROM RADIO TO TELEVISION

John Keir Cross

When this article was published in Spring 1952 television was still a new market for authors and the BBC monopoly had not yet been challenged. John Keir Cross was responding to the editor's invitation to discuss 'the differences between writing for sound and vision broadcasting'.

I'VE BEEN LUCKY enough to have had some fifteen years of fairly steady, fairly voluminous radio writing of all kinds; and if I haven't, in the past few, submitted quite as much to television as perhaps for my own future good I ought, it has been because (without any preciosity, you must believe) as a Calvin-conscienced Scot I haven't felt totally *ready*. That indicates difference at the outset; for the writers who are more likely to turn to television than most others, I'd suggest, are those who see a sizeable part of their present means of livelihood disappearing and this new thing developing. If it were only a matter of adding simple vision to work at present conceived for sound why, for our purse's sake we'd be at it this moment.... But it is not as easy as that – not a matter of switching from one medium to another.... There are differences – a host; and at this moment in 1952 the prime of them is that television *is* the new thing, and sound radio ('blind radio' as they call it – or even 'steam radio') is the established. Sound has its set conventions, its trained public, its comprehensible bag of tricks; but not television – yet.

Somebody at Broadcasting House the other day made the stunning pronouncement, when I was arguing over some question of relative payments for two shows – one for steam, the other for (presumably) jet-propelled radio – that in fact it was more difficult to write for sound than for vision; and elaborated in a long disquisition, when he saw the look of bewilderment on me, on communication being easier when the audience could see as well as hear. I suppose that in a large way the argument is tenable enough – although I swear it doesn't chime with the experience of most of us who have tried both mediums. Given the fact that sound and vision had both come into existence simultaneously – say last year, six months ago; then most of us – professional writers tackling the two new markets – might indeed find sound more tricky to master in some of its basic principles, would have to go through all the old wearinesses of Narrators One and Two before developing the self-contained convention which had its beginnings in the work of Tyrone Guthrie and Lance Sieveking more than twenty years ago. But the truth is that Guthrie and Sieveking did set the pace all that time past; and new radio writers nowadays find a whole technique awaiting – it has passed into common professional experience, is something that although it is capable of still further development, has its main principles truly downlaid. It is not so yet with television – the Guthries have not yet appeared. We are, in fact, at this moment, all potential Guthries (in this one sense); and so – natural geniuses always excepted – find it in practice, I suggest, not only 'different' but much more difficult to write for vision than for sound. . . .

And the situation here and now, in 1952 – and still for long enough to come – is complicated even further by a host of purely mechanical considerations at Alexandra Palace and Lime Grove which never worried the pioneers at Savoy Hill and Broadcasting House. They had, of course, their early struggles with imperfect microphones, with crude recording gear and so on; but these are nothing to the technical horrors of television production – of the more complex mechanics of a vision show. . . . Many of them may disappear as television develops its resources; but even at the best, I believe, there will still be more wrighting in vision and more writing in sound.

Of course the stage playwright is equally handicapped by the physical capabilities of his cast – and contrives, therefore, to tell his story in blocks of action. So must the telvision playwright, in a way that concerns his radio playwriter colleague not at all. Yet he must contrive even further – he must contrive the additional illusion that he is *not* contriving in such blocks of action; for by its nature, by its very shape, its proportions, its coloration even, the television screen is virtually the cinema screen: it plays to a public educated by this time to accept, even to *require* (if unconsciously, perhaps) the full fluidity of the cinema, which is as fluid as sound radio – even the spaciousness of the cinema, its largeness of canvas quite impossible to achieve on the crowded sets of even the biggest imaginable television studio. Nor would it be enough to seek an answer in filming specially for television, for not only is that a kind of cheating, but it destroys the very strength of the medium – its immediacy. . . .

The Guthrie-to-come may establish finally a style which, peculiar to television, still does keep all the necessary pictorial mobility while never overstraining the physical capabilities of on-the-spot actors, scene-shifters and camera-men. In twenty years' time, when this has been done, the ordinary competent writer we started off with will find a convention waiting for him to which he can fit his own ideas, as at the moment is the case in sound. But until then we must embrace all the limitations of the newer medium and wrestle with them somewhat blindly over and above our natural wrestling with our basic story ideas. And the obvious fact is that no matter what future improvements on present makeshifts there may be, there will always be required this extra more elaborate planning in writing for vision (in wrighting for vision). It will need more skilled carpentry even than radio writing does.

It is no bad thing, of course – it is, in fact, an immense stimulus to come across something in our time which is not cut and dried, which requires as much contributive creative development from all of us as the early cinema and radio pioneer craftsmen had to exercise. So the challenge is there and there is no doubt that sooner or later we shall rise to it – as many of us are already doing and even have done. But here, at the tail end, is the one true controversial issue – which must be touched on: the one true practical difference after all (in another sense) between writing for the two mediums that concerns that same ordinary, competent professional writer. . . .

It is a lamentable fact that some [of the BBC administration] do not comprehend even now that writing for any kind of broadcasting is a profession. Somebody else at Broadcasting House once made to an established author in my presence the astonishing statement, in a tone of complete shocked surprise: 'But we don't *expect* authors to *make a living* from writing for us! – it's only a sideline for them, you know. . . .' So the true gesture that can be made is for all of them . . . to realize that to most ordinary professional writers (and they are the people they must cozen, not the Big Boys, for television will become as hungry as sound is now and there won't be enough of the Big Boys to go round) – to most of these ordinary competent writers the technique of the new medium is difficult to learn, takes time to learn and even when it is learned will still be difficult to exercise – will always, in one aspect alone, take more time to exercise, because of that extra planning I mentioned. It is all, in fact, more 'different' than they at present realize; for to many of them television plainly only *is* another kind of broadcasting in the old comfortable way they understand it – is a kind of department.

260

I need hardly overtly state, I think, that one of the things I am driving at is that there will have to be more cash forthcoming – they will have to assess the two mediums differently. They do, at the moment, give a little more cash ('for working in the television medium' as the contract forms say). Yet there are certain unprofessional inhibitions on the doling out of this avuncular extra – and even then, in practice, and taking the long view, it is nothing like enough. They may not have the cash – but it is their problem to find more for this basic *wrighting* they do so desperately need, not ours. Our problem is to earn an adequate return for work done. . . . Even apart from cash, there are many contractual aspects of television which are based too closely on the principles fought for in the past to deal fairly with sound. . . .

I believe that the powers that be (or may be) will sooner or later have to set to building a professional class of television writers – to make it worth an author's while to study and work for the medium even to the exclusion of all else from his life, not only as a 'sideline'. We may all, in the bland assumption of too many of *them*, be pioneers, charged romantically with the high nobility of our mission; but we were fully qualified farmers before we went west – and it is they, in final sooth, who want the new territory worked over and developed. What are needed, in short, are pioneer administrators as well as pioneer craftsmen: for there are indeed differences between serving the two mediums – in other fields than in writing for them.

. . . .

Television *needs* writers. Television needs *writers*. Needs them as the cinema needs them. Needs them more than 'sound' radio needs them. Needs them so that television can become itself, can begin to grow to full stature, can begin to cease to look like an imitation of other media. It needs them in drama, in documentary, in revues, in musical comedy, in

261

If you are a writer and interested, may I please ask you not to write in immediately saying (as many people have done), 'I want to write for television. May I come and see some productions in the studios?' That can certainly be arranged if you persist, but I shall try hard to discourage you. The first thing to do, the essential and inescapable thing, is to look at television, to look at it over a period of three months, as often as possible. That is a hard thing, even a dangerous thing, to say. I wish I had not to say it. However, there are a lot of people who have not seen television, and a lot of writers are among them. . . . How can a writer appreciate television's aims and ambitions, its strengths and weaknesses, its limitations and possibilities, its present standards and facilities, unless he looks at it, stares at it? And because the evening transmission time is limited to two hours, he must look a long time before he sees a sufficient number in each of the programme categories to enable his pen to begin to write smoothly for any one of them.

> Cecil McGivern, BBC Controller of Television
> Programmes, introducing his article
> "Television Needs Writers', Winter 1950

THE BBC TRADITION

J.B. Priestley

In Autumn 1966 The Author *published a special section on 'Radio and the Writer' from which we take this extract.*

IT ALL BEGAN badly for writers and talkers on the air. I know this because I can well remember the Old Savoy Hill days. You were expected then to write or talk on the cheap because you were offered a large audience and any broadcast would be good publicity. This seemed to me a bad argument. A large audience should pay handsomely. And writers with any self-respect should not do things for the sake of publicity. They should not enter the world of advertising agencies. And a great public corporation should not use publicity as a bargaining point.

I am not saying this attitude was maintained down the years. What I am saying is that negotiations with writers came to be haunted by a bad tradition and usually took place in a bad atmosphere. Writers were expected to be cheap even when singers, fiddlers and comics came dear. And it wasn't understood – isn't fully understood to this day – that bargain-price writing makes a dubious foundation on which to erect expensive programmes. No good writing, no good programme – no matter how much talent is commanded after the scripts are done. Of course, underpaid writing may still be fine work; but it is much easier to demand good writing, and to make sure it *is* good, when fees are so handsome that they make tempting prizes. Would scripts be

263

much better if all fees were trebled next week? Certainly they would.

The BBC has been bedevilled by the sheer size of its organization and operations. If it had to give contracts to only ten writers, I am sure it would treat those writers as they ought to be treated – as *artists* and not as journeymen and sausage-makers. Because there aren't ten of them but a hundred, two hundred, three hundred, this doesn't mean that writers have turned into quite different *kinds* of people, so many verbal bricklayers or roadmen.

It may be objected that these very writers, working through their Radiowriters' Association, have been trying desperately hard to fix minimum fees. This is because existing fees, when the cost of living is taken into account, are shockingly bad. And why are they so bad? Because – and here I return to my main argument – the BBC wishes to spend as little as possible on writers and writing. If money can be saved, then save it on *them*. They are the soft spot that can be squeezed. No union will bring them out on strike. There is no competitive radio network, of any size, to offer them better terms. So it's take-it-or-leave-it. And behind this attitude, stiffening it, is the belief, a thoroughly sound, decent English belief, that writers and writing *don't really matter*.

THIRTY YEARS ON

Allan Prior

In Autumn 1983 The Author *published an informal report by Allan Prior on writing for television, which he had been doing with some regularity since the mid-1950s. His article was called* 'Writing for the One-eyed Monster'.

IN 1956 I WAS beginning to write regularly for television, and so I wrote a novel about it, *The One-eyed Monster*. My publisher was not enthusiastic about the subject, of which he knew nothing, and nobody was more surprised than he was when it went into six languages, was serialized in British and German magazines, television adaptations of it were shown in Italy, Germany and on the famous 'Armchair Theatre', and it became a sort of cult book. I was a bit surprised myself, but I shouldn't have been. Television had already become *the* popular medium, it was swallowing up movies, theatre, and the glossy news magazines in large gulps and it was fast converting Fleet Street from a news-gathering machine into a bunch of after-the-event commentators, television having shown everything worth seeing the day before.

Not that I approved of any of this. I didn't. I'd started out to write nothing but novels (I've managed only fourteen) but had discovered I could write drama, and television was there. The point was, it wasn't only swallowing the older print-and-photo mediums, it was gobbling up actors and directors and writers, too. When I found myself writing three *Z Cars* episodes in ten days, I knew I was in the feared jaws of the Monster myself.

The news from the front line in television is that it has changed. But not much.

Example: I'm currently writing, for the first time since the middle sixties, a trilogy of television plays (for Scottish Television). In the sixties I had (as I have now) three one-hour slots, a cast list that must not get out of hand, i.e., no more than, say, eight actors. If you see twenty speaking parts in an hour play, you know you're looking at a novice dramatist. Then, as now, I'm writing to (at top) six studio 'sets' and (top) fifteen minutes of film per episode, better say twelve. The subjects, in both cases, are working class: no, *not* more sociological–Marxist tracts, I hasten to add. In the sixties I was writing about three people working on the Golden Mile at Blackpool. The trilogy I'm writing now is about a bookie in Sauchiehall Street, Glasgow. As it happens, I know a bit about both.

So, the second thing that hasn't changed: television drama still isn't the theatre and it isn't novels. At its best, it's in the street. At its worst, it's in Hampstead. So, if any advice is ever worth giving, mine would be: if you haven't got, and don't enjoy, the common touch, leave television writing well alone!

Producers in television, who have to sell your ideas to their programme controllers, may wistfully wish to do plays and series about the sort of people they know will interest the readers of the *Guardian*; but in the end they incline (for the sake not just of the mortgage, but of their huge audience) to go for subjects that are, in some kind of way, popular, of common interest. You might say, like hanging? You wouldn't be far wrong.

Say it to any besandalled, bejeaned and blow-waved producer in his workingman's shirt (from Blade's or Gieves) and he would nod, look morosely out of his window over whatever complex he is currently at (producers and directors change seats faster than airline pilots, whom they much resemble in all sorts of ways) and muse, 'Yeah. Great. But how could we *do* it, man? I mean, *how?*'

Television is in the bums-on-seats game. So any writer going to one of the ITV companies or the BBC with an idea for anything at all (and for most writers that means drama) should think, first off: will this vast amorphous audience be interested?

Now, there *is* a difference: away from the series and serials and adaptations of novels (to which I'll return) there is a market for up-market drama à la Dennis Potter. It lives exclusively at the BBC, who don't really care if *Pennies from Heaven* started with eight million people watching it and finished with less than two. So what, the critics loved it! You *can* go there with your fashionable agin-the-Establishment-trendy-liberal play. Sorry to put it like that, but you know what I mean!

That *is* new. In the sixties even the plays had to be *popular*. I used to write plays for ABC's 'Armchair Theatre' that had audiences of seventeen millions on a Sunday evening, one in every three persons in these islands. Now, if a play gets an audience of six millions everybody is manic with delight. The bad sociological dramas (like a long, grey series) have – almost – dished the popular play. Not quite, however. If a writer *looks* at the schedules (and any working television dramatist does, every week) he'll know where to send his play, and more importantly, to whom.

Producers are the people to talk to. Or write to, if you must. In the sixties and even the early seventies (when most producers had come to television from the theatre, or the movies, or even the war) you had direct access to somebody who knew something about the world outside telvision. Now, few do. They are television creatures, and know what was on last night. Or maybe last week. A week is, indeed, a long time in television. So, that has changed, and with the change has come that dreaded creature, the script editor.

267

He's been around in drama since Sidney Newman imported him from Canada in the sixties. But I never discussed my *Z Cars* scripts with any editor, not in the original series. I just wrote them. *Z Cars* was the fruit of the collaboration of two writers (Troy Kennedy Martin and myself) and a director, John McGrath. That was *it*. The rest was admin and back-up.

It couldn't happen now. The editor looms over the writer, almost everywhere. As one writer once said to me, 'Television is the only business where a beginner (and lots of script editors *are* beginners, on their way to being producers) actually tell specialists who earn six times what they do, how to do a thing.'

He was absolutely right. But there are some series where you *have* to have an editor – the BBC has an editor on every show, even original plays: what, for God's sake, has an *editor* to contribute to an original play? Really it's just something that got out of hand, in the way of all big organizations. In practice, what the editor does is to remove from the producer the necessity of thinking about 'stories', something that normally he's supremely ill equipped to do anyway. Few producers would agree with that, and I apologize to all my friends, but do not retract a word. I don't tell them who to cast, they shouldn't tell me what or how to write. Strangely, few see it that way!

One thing that hasn't changed: everybody is a writer. That is news no professional writer will be surprised to hear.

Other things that *have* changed: there are very few truly 'contemporary' series on the box. And most prestige drama is now on film. It's wildly expensive (you have to take costume girls and make-up girls along even if you don't *need* them, would you believe it?) but it doesn't take anything like the actual writing *ability* a studio drama takes. Film always *looks* 50 per cent better than your script: and studio (with its unavoidable overlit, stagey theatrical style) looks 50 per cent *worse*.

So that's new. We used to have OBs – i.e., Outside Broadcast Units – for drama sometimes. Never film. I have, of course, written drama on film, and, frankly, it's a breeze. You get what you ask for. A field? OK. A pit-head? Fine. A volcano? No trouble. In studio drama, you get a *room*. Interior. Overlit. The actors all neat and tidy and the actresses all with super hairdos. It's artistic *murder*. But it's there. The vast electronic studios are there, at White City and wherever. They *have* to be used. It's that most powerful of all fellows, Mr Precedent, operating.

Has television writing itself – the act of doing it – changed much, then, since the early days of *Z Cars*? Probably not a lot, any more than any kind of writing has changed. Fashions have changed. Some techniques have changed. Some kinds of financing have changed. Co-productions are the order of the day, since television went international. Yet that doesn't really affect the writer. There are a lot more dramatizations (usually of creaky old costume epics of the thirties, forties and fifties) but few novelists or short-story writers are asked to adapt them. They go to the old hands who do nothing else. I did one of the earliest of the so-called classic serials, Louis Golding's *Magnolia Street*, a wonderful, gutsy, original novel. I did it because I loved it, and wanted other people, who'd never read it, to enjoy it, too.

That hasn't changed. Television gets, headily, to the millions. There is this terrific First Night. The thing to remember: it's all there is.

So, exciting it is, and a profession no more than it ever was, for sensitive, retiring souls. A writer has to be ready, in television, to defend his play against the well-meaning attacks of producers, actors, script editors, and everybody else in sight. The thing is not to argue, but to win. If you stand firm, they usually give way.

Now for the one thing that is vastly different. There's a lot less drama than there was: only two-thirds of the drama there was ten years ago.

It's very expensive (£150,000 per hour, at its cheapest) and rumours that there's going to be even less – almost certainly true – abound in the places, usually bars, where practising writers, directors, producers, editors, actors meet. So the prevailing mood is, let's play safe, we have millions of money invested, we have co-production partners. 'A *new* writer to do some of the scripts? Are you bloody mad, Allan?'

So, leaving aside the hotted-up journalism and the cretinous sit-coms and talking only about television drama, which has been the best thing television has given us, the best of it better than anything done in the theatre over the last twenty years (of course, a lot of it has been awful, too) one can sum up by saying: it's the same tough act of selling and creation as it ever was, and although the door isn't firmly shut against new writers, because there are dozens of television writers who write only two or three scripts a year (there are *hundreds* in the Writers' Guild) it is still harder now, I think, to make a big *name* and impact than it was. But then, it's always been hard to make a big name and impact anywhere.

For myself, I have always loved writing for television, despite its pitfalls and wayward foolishness, because I like actors and delight in having my lines spoken. It's anarchic sometimes, but it makes a nice change from the orderliness of prose, sitting to set hours, writing a novel in a room. I can't say which is best to do – television plays are shouts in the street, a novel is a whisper in the ear. One answers to both calls.

But, dear colleague, if you don't hear the clarion call to write television drama loud and clear, stay away. It is no game for fainthearts, then as now. It's still that same old, bloody One-eyed Monster.

INTO THE LABYRINTH

In the Spring issue of 1980 Doris Lessing's article 'My First Book' opened an occasional series, from which we also republish contributions by Anthony Burgess (Summer 1981), William Golding (Autumn 1981) and Rosamond Lehmann (Summer 1983). Some years earlier, in Spring 1967, Tom Stoppard had described, wryly, the background to the play that was to launch his theatrical career: his article is also reproduced below.

Writing a book is like making a compost heap, piling in all the sweepings, peelings, old flowers, blood and garbage of life. Frustrations and failures become fertilizer, and little potato peelings sprout new shoots, peach seeds become saplings, cherry trees need tender transplanting, plots and subplots rise out of the compost, not from the earth but from the dark recess of contemplated experience. Odours, fragrances, smells, stinks come to the nostrils of the mind unbidden, and everything goes into a book.

Beatrice Levin, 'The Writer in the Horseradish',
Autumn 1978

Doris Lessing

WHEN I WAS FOURTEEN I was a nursemaid for two years in Salisbury, Rhodesia. Now I would be called an au pair girl. I wrote stories and watched events that could make novels; I tested and tasted words. Remember, when you come to describe so-and-so, these are the words for it. Then I went back to the farm and wrote two novels. One was a comedy of manners: Salisbury social life. The other I think was satirical, but I could not read it back. It had been written at high speed in pencil. Thus I learned never to become inspired unless somewhere near a typewriter.

While I was married and having babies I was always hatching some idea, and I began and half finished novels. One, which got to the second draft stage, was shown to my then sister-in-law, a woman with a life so sad she soon died of it, but she said the book was morbid. When I put myself back into my then state of mind, I know there were many things I wanted to do, as much as, more than, to write. I hungered, I yearned, for experience, for travel, for movement, to get out of Rhodesia. But that was the war: it was the war that formed us, even when we were not actually in it.

I remember the suddenness of how it struck me that I described myself as a writer, and other people did – but where was the evidence? Half a dozen stories published in South Africa, some bad verse, and rejection slips from England? Quite a few people I knew said they were, or would be, writers and could write well. It is my belief that

273

talent is plentiful, and that what is lacking is staying power. I was shorthand typist and dogsbody for a legal firm. I went into my boss and said I was giving notice to write a novel. His look was kindly. I was then faced with writing a novel. What novel? How could I be a writer without a burning need to write this rather than that? Everything I saw and touched seemed the starting point for a story. I had kept a newspaper cutting about a black man murdering a white woman. No motive! I had spent years wondering why black servants did not murder neurotic, nagging, contemptuous housewives. Soon I was able to see those women as pathetic. You write your way into being more human, I think.

I had an infant and was, with my husband, a social focus for a number of young people more or less left wing. I was part-time typist for Hansard and for Government Commissions. This is an obsolete job. You typed extremely fast while the shorthand writer dictated. I enjoyed it. It was also useful. From the Commission on the Recruitment of Native Labour I gathered facts which, when I used them in my work, the Rhodesian authorities said were untrue. I also learned why Government Commissions are usually ineffective.

It was not hard to write my first novel, once I had cleared a space around myself. I remember my agreeable surprise that I had a quarter of it done, then a half, then it was finished. It was despatched to London publishers. This was before airmail was reintroduced after the war. Six weeks' train and boat-time to England, then the publishers kept it their usual inexcusable time, then six weeks' boat- and train-time back. The train took five days from Cape Town to Salisbury. This was a most valuable lesson in acquiring inner patience, and that calculated obstinacy which I regard as any writer's most valuable asset. The other hard thing was advice from friends. Of all the obstacles a writer has to surmount, this is the worst, I think. If the self-elected committee are your loving friends, whom you admire for other reasons, then it is hard indeed. Am I saying advice is never good? I can say I have had good advice about *how*, but never about *what*, to write.

I looked carefully at the much rejected *Grass*. It consisted of an inner subplot, embedded in a mass which I threw away. (I have nearly always destroyed what has not come off, and have not regretted it.) The discarded two-thirds was based on one of the great perennial comic ideas. A young idealistic Englishman fresh from university, stuffed with scientific and *true* ideas about race, class, religion and so forth, arrives in Rhodesia, and, no, he does not either leave, or change himself to fit his new surroundings. He sticks it out, challenging everything around him, with the sincere and radiant conviction of this rectitude. I think this character was influenced by *The Idiot*. I was soaked in Dostoevsky. (Also Proust.) I switched the end about, changed the young Englishman, and there was *The Grass is Singing*.

A Johannesburg friend got me a South African publisher. He was the first of the godmothers. Every first novel acquires godparents who thereafter say: 'It was because of me.' This is quite apart from the way established writers look after new ones: an essential, and sometimes unnoticed, part of the literary machine. I was, and remain, grateful to this man who helped me at my worst time. In South Africa had just been published a novel, now forgotten, called, I think, *The Expiring Frog*, which had sold well in America. This publisher hoped to do the same with mine.

I signed a contract. Came to England. While surviving in precarious ways I sent short stories to Curtis Brown. Juliet O'Hea wrote to say, 'Did I have a novel?' Yes, but it was contracted to a South African publisher. Why hadn't it been published, she wanted to know. Well, why hadn't it? And why hadn't I made a fuss? But what about the helplessness of the unpublished who have nothing to base a fight on but a potential? No, I have not, believe me, I have *not*, forgotten that helplessness. But what protects is precisely the passivity that can seem a weakness, and is, sometimes, but can be, as well, a useful patience, the ability to wait. Juliet O'Hea said the contract amounted to crookery, got me out of it, and sold *The Grass* at once to Michael Joseph. The reader who liked it there was Pamela Hansford Johnson. About Juliet, I can only hope they make them like that now, plentifully, for the sake of beginning writers. She believed that a writer who had sold only a short story or an unprofitable novel should get as much time and attention as the famous and the profitable. And that young writers should stand firm on what they are.

I remember when I had no money at all, I was being tempted – the accurate word – by a now defunct newspaper, the *Daily Graphic*, to write a series of articles supporting hanging, flogging, racialism, etc. They offered money that would solve all my problems for years. I was not likely to give in, but it was nice to have Juliet saying, 'Certainly *not*.' And when an honourable and prestigious New York publishing firm said they would publish the book if I changed the end to an explicit rape, because 'this would be in accordance with the mores of the country', she backed me up: Certainly *not*.

Luckily for me I was ignorant about the economics of the book business, and did not know it was impossible to live on what you earn. I gave up a job as a secretary on the basis of a £150 advance. When Michael Joseph rang me up several times to say the book was being reprinted before publication, I was unimpressed, because I thought this happened to everyone. This was a good thing. I was getting on with my work, and did not fall into one of the worst of the traps, particularly bad for provincials and colonials, that is set by the emotion: 'At last I am being welcomed in by my peers, by lovely literature.' From this embrace some never emerge again, and ordinary life sees them not.

The book did well for a first novel. This was partly luck, which should never be left out of account. Mine was the second book published here about Southern Africa, the first being *Cry the Beloved Country*. Five years later reviewers might have said: 'Another book about the colour bore.' I quote. It was hard going for about ten years. But I am not a worrier about money, and easily do without things if I have to. Also a friend helped by letting me pile up rent till I could pay, and I was lent money – once by someone I did not even know. It arrived in the post.

The reviews were on the whole good. They did not affect me. The long process of sticking it out in Rhodesia gave me a tough skin, or, if you like, a hard core, at any rate, a perspective. Colonials are fortunate in being both inside a culture and outside it in a way that enables us to see certain processes clearly. Undue reverence is not one of our faults. I am sad when I see young writers being affected by reviews. *Who writes them?* You can *occasionally* get useful advice from reviews, but you can *always* learn a great deal about a current literary climate.

Advice to young writers? Always the same advice: learn to trust your own judgement, learn inner independence, learn to trust that time will sort good from bad – including your own bad. Do not pay attention to current literary modes, for they can be observed changing, sometimes overnight. Remember that the reviewer who dismissed you with a sneer will, if the book is a success, greet you five years later with: 'How much I did enjoy that book!' Remember that from the moment a book is accepted the pressures start to get you to lecture, to give seminars, to travel to conferences, to play parlour games on television, to do everything and anything but write.

You will have to do some of these things. Publicity of this sort is an aspect of the sales departments of the publishing houses. Some publishers now will take a book only if there is a clause in the contract that you will agree to 'promote' the book on television and so forth. In other words, if you agree to sell your personality. The only antidote is steadily to insist on calling things by their proper names, and to be clear in your mind about what you are doing. Nine-tenths of these pressures will deplete that part of yourself that feeds the precarious entity, the writer. Learn to say no, no, no, no, as much as you can. Learn what feeds energy into you, and what drains you. Learn to watch, to harbour, to make, energy. Energy is our capital.

And it does no harm to repeat, as often as you can, 'Without me the literary industry would not exist: the publishers, the agents, the sub-agents, the sub-sub-agents, the accountants, the libel lawyers, the departments of literature, the professors, the theses, the books of criticism, the reviewers, the book pages – all this vast and proliferating edifice is because of this small, patronized, put-down and underpaid person.'

Anthony Burgess

I NEVER HAD ANY ambition as a writer. If, at the university, I became involved in the study of English and its literature, this was because, having failed in physics in the old School Certificate examination, I was not permitted to pursue a course in music. I knew about books but, up to the age of thirty-six, I still hoped to be a distinguished musician. It was while I was scoring a work for large orchestra in, I think, the year 1953, that I was visited by a spasm of envy for writers. I had to fill in thirty staves of full score to produce about five seconds of sound (if the work should ever reach the stage of being accepted, its parts copied, its survival at rehearsal, its release from the auditory imagination and launching at real if disregarding ears); the author dealt in pure monody, the one line of typescript at a time, and as soon as the work got on to paper it was already, in a sense, being performed. So I took time off from my symphony and wrote a little novel. I found the work easy and refreshing. I enjoyed creating characters and making them move about and clash with each other. I enjoyed spinning words: it was rather like creating music but far less fatiguing. Having written this little book I sent it off to Heinemann. I admired the novels of Graham Greene and knew he was a Heinemann author. So Heinemann it was. I then forgot about the novel and got back to my colossal orchestral score, reflecting on an interesting

279

if minor truth – that music manuscript paper cost a great deal more than typing paper.

To my surprise I received a letter from the chief editor of Heinemann, asking me to drop in for a chat. I was living in the Midlands and could not afford the fare to London and back, but by chance I was also invited to visit the Colonial Office in Great Smith Street to discuss the possibility of a job in Malaya, and the Colonial Office was very willing to pay my fare. Thus I was able also to go to Heinemann.

My first little novel was not, in fact, accepted for publication, but I was encouraged to go on writing. I went back home to meet a great wave of the guilt which periodically visits British renegade Catholics, and I was inspired to write a novel about a guilty Catholic schoolmaster, rather like myself, living in the soggy Midlands. I sent this novel off to Heinemann and got a letter not merely of rejection but of vituperation. The novel was nothing more than a great wave of guilt of the kind which periodically visits British renegade Catholics. I said to hell and went off to Malaya. There I wrote music based on Malayan themes and rhythms. I also wrote a novel about Malaya called *Time for a Tiger*. There was guilt in this, but not of the renegade Catholic kind, and the work was accepted for publication. It sold rather well and was decently reviewed. I think that its mild success had more to do with its exotic subject-matter than any distinction the writing and structure may have possessed. Signing a contract for it (the advance was all of fifty pounds) I found myself signing also for other books, not yet written and perhaps never to be written. Encouraged by publication, I was not inclined to write any more words: I had shown that I could do it and that was all that mattered. I got on with a more important task – the composition of a symphony to celebrate forthcoming Malayan Independence. It was entitled *Simfoni Merdeka*. It was sent to the appropriate department in Kuala Lumpur and there rejected. To hell. I would write another novel.

I wrote a number of novels while in Malaya and Borneo. Invalided out of the Colonial Service with a suspected cerebral tumour, unable to get a job in Britain, I became a professional novelist because I knew no other way of making a living. It was not much of a living; it never is. But that is not the point of the discourse. The point is my first novel. Which was my first novel – the one that was published and called this promising first novel, or the two others, or one of them, which were rejected? Of these two I had better say, for the record, that both were eventually published. The one previously rejected with vituperation was accepted by the same editor and now called good. The other one, the real first, came out with another publisher about ten years after my first submitting it. Waste is a terrible thing. Nothing, you see, was wasted.

That first novel (the first to be published, I mean) is still sound after twenty-five years, but I do not now find it easy reading: too many faults of form and errors of style. I was forced into rereading it last year when my wife was translating it into Italian and occasionally needed help, and I did not object because here at least was a chance to improve it: the Italian is better than the English and, in general, I would say that most of the translations I have been able to supervise are better than the originals. This should not be but is so. Joyce was sure that the *Finnegans Wake* he was translating into French was going to be superior to that laborious Eurish.

One thing I learned about my first novel was what all the reviewers thought of it, from Little Rock to Broken Hill, for I subscribed to a press-cutting agency, a thing I have not done since. I learned thus, what I have had no occasion to unlearn, that reviewers do not read books with much care, and that their profession is more given to stupidity and malice and literary ignorance even than the profession of novelist. I have a character in that book who is a police-lieutenant during the Malayan Emergency, but the blurb turned him into a sergeant, presumably because the blurb writer could not reconcile his rough demotic speech with the rank I gave him. All the reviewers referred to him as a police sergeant, except one, who crossly asked: 'Why can't Mr Burgess make up his mind as to what rank this character possesses?' It was the fashion in those days to call everybody an angry young man and I, though thirty-seven, had to become one too. The book, however, is humorous rather than angry, and its humour is probably its main virtue. I discovered I was a funny writer, and I had never seen myself as anything but a creature of gloom and sobriety.

Young writers looking forward to the publication of your first novels, remember this: you will never again know the joy of authorship; there is no greater pleasure in life than unwrapping your first proof copy. These words are yours; they are not merely in print, they are in a book, and they share the dubious sempiternality of the First Folio (which Shakespeare never saw and would not have given a damn about it if he had; he would certainly not have been keen on correcting the proofs: too much else to be done – land-buying and litigation and getting his daughter Judith married). If you have not yet started writing your first novel, consider it as a projected singleton, a work to be made as good as possible, a work compressing your entire personality into 200-odd pages, a work not to be followed by any other. One book is enough for anyone, but unfortunately some of us have to write far more in order to pay the rent and the gas bill. But there is nothing in this work of the pleasure we knew when we were hopeful and smelt the ink of our first page proofs.

William Golding

In 1934 Messrs Macmillan published, among their shilling series of 'Contemporary Poets', *Poems* by W.G. Golding. It ran to thirty-four pages, and the verses ranged from four lines to twenty-eight. Today, in 1981, the book has been on offer in the United States at 4,000 dollars. This is nothing but value by association.

I have had a lifelong love of rhythm, sound and, in particular, rhyme. At my dame school there was a thing called 'recitation' where each age, from six to ten years old, stood up in turn and said the piece they had learned by rote. I learned everybody else's piece as well as my own, by listening. I had in a developed degree the 'flypaper memory' of childhood and never forgot what I had heard once. I had, too, a direct appreciation that verse was an important deed, though of course I never thought to formulate the feeling and probably could not have done so. Doctor Foster went to Gloucester and it was deliriously funny that he should take *that* name to *that* place, and quite appropriate that he should step into a puddle deeper than puddle ever was in a world gone clownish. And then – *Boot, saddle, to horse and away* was more of a rush than Brooklands, or fighter planes flying at more than a hundred miles an hour. Then, *Who will* stand *on either* hand *and keep the bridge?* I knew that I wouldn't stand on either hand but I could recognize and enjoy someone else's courage.

And so on. Of course, the change came with the ugly

283

word, that rearrangement of personality, additions of emotion, perception, joy, pain. Poetry began to speak to the whole man or boy, rather. My first *adult* appreciation at thirteen or fourteen was of the more accessible sonnets of Shakespeare. *Shall I compare thee*, of course, and perhaps another half-dozen, together with the songs. I began to scribble after that – scribble at verse, I mean, for I had always been a scribbler of prose.

These verses were bits of lyric. I had a Wordsworthian belief in the primacy of the lyric. The lyric could be short and simple – the simpler the better. It is easier, on the whole, to read the poetry of a European language than its prose. Except in aberrations like metaphysical poetry, the ideas, proclamations, celebrations, invocations, are not confused and detained by any close reasoning. I did not care for close reasoning. It was too much like work.

I quite early came to understand that poetry was a matter of what I will call *interior stance*. A man was either swept into that stance or willed himself into it. It might be called, in the case of the adolescent lyricist, the *vocative stance*. In my own case the ohs and ahs were fervent. Nevertheless though Wordsworth would have condemned my habit of invoking the mighty dead rather than the living he would have recognized the stance, as would most of the Romantics. It was to be many years later that I read, and at last understood, Cleanth Brooks's assessment of the stance, where he points out how narrowly it limited the feelings and subjects thought worthy of poetry.

What had I that gave me any genuine relationship to the job? It was a small thing, I believe, and not altogether helpful. I passionately enjoyed, lengthily savoured the *phrase*. It might not be *a jewel five words long* and was more likely to be two words only, a noun with attendant adjective. It would be a phrase that re-created by some magic the phenomenon that lay under its hand. This kind of phrase was the opposite of the Homeric epithet which, having done its first work of evocation, was thereafter repeated as a moment of rest for the listener and was finally assimilated to the noun and became an accepted part of it. My phrases were not repeated *multitudinous sea*, 'anerithmon gelasma', *neiges d'antan, dew-dabbled poppies*! These were (and are) more precious than stamps or birds' eggs or crystals or jewels. Out of *Thyrsis whose sweet art hath oft delayed the huddling brook to hear his madrigale*, my ear and eye and imagination took 'huddling brook' and saw (as it still sees) the very thing conjured by the words.

Let me call such a phrase a 'unit'. The capacity to invent a unit which was at first sight an advantage was in fact a hindrance when I came to essay extended verses. The verses tended to huddle like the brook rather than flow. They became so dense as to be opaque. They clotted rather than formed round the unit. Combined with the *vocative stance* they permitted no more than a brief comment on some idea so approachable, so universal as to be commonplace. Spring is coming or here or over, winter is about somewhere, how sweetly sad autumn is, how heavy summer by comparison. I was conscious that I said nothing but was uneasily preoccupied with how I said it.

Now this was particularly difficult at a time when – whether the word was current or not – a poet was supposed to be closely 'engaged' to social questions. I was quite disengaged, bar a very mild feeling which I got from my parents that the Labour Party was Our Side. I lacked the generosity of spirit that would give all – not merely life but writing too! – for the betterment of mankind. I was stuck with the unit. Even to think of getting the two words apart for alternative use in the same poem created in me a sympathetic muscular tension as if I were using chest developers. Indeed, to tear them apart would have violated the only thing I had. What was lacking in me – though I may have developed it later – was a certain mobility of outlook, the power to walk round the back and see the thing from the other side, to walk away from and see it in relation to what was all around. I could see what short verses were, but not what by alteration and perhaps extension they might become. I lacked the attitude of the chess master, who, finding a good move, is not content, but looks for a better one. I have always been a curious mixture of conservative and anarchist. Translated into an attitude towards verse-making this means either being content with a minimal result or destroying the thing petulantly.

Today, some of my units seem less jewels than pebbles; but after all, a pebble is a jewel of a sort. To take an example, the phrase 'twisted violets' seemed to me to have the proper magical immediacy of evocation though it has not much power over my mind now. If there is a concordance to the sort of poetry which contents adolescents I might well find that the phrase was not my own, for such associations of adjective and noun stick subliminally like advertisements. I search my mind for a few moments and come up with *violet-embroider'd dale, sweet as Cytherea's eyelids*, and *the year's first violet white and lonely* though there must be hundreds more. Perhaps I *was* the first man who ever put *twisted* and *violet* together!

This preoccupation with the minutiae of the craft was interrupted and now and then subsumed in another experience more like true eloquence – not I mean in value but in method. There were moments when a positive and coherent thought rose up with emotion and brought both rhyme and metre – it seemed in that order – to the surface of my mind. It was my first meeting with the mystery of the mind as not so much as giving *to* airy nothing a local habitation as creating *out* of airy nothing. It was the unconscious (of which I had not heard) triggered by emotion – hardly to be distinguished from the involuntary phrases, ejaculations, admonishments, prayers, runes and spells that can be heard from the lips of a man talking, as we say, to himself. I will make a watery comparison and liken myself to a pipe furred

with phrases that occasionally allowed squirts of liquid past
to demonstrate that the tube was almost wholly blocked.

Clearly, if the cork could be taken out or the fur removed
there would be some flow. I experienced it once, a remarkable
example of how pure the flow could be – pure, as it were, in
terms of hydrodynamics rather than in the intrinsic value of
the resultant fluid. I wanted to go back to Cornwall and the
sea but was in Wiltshire. While walking on the Marlborough
Downs where now there is a memorial stone to Edward
Thomas, Alfred Williams (the 'railway poet') and Charles
Hamilton Sorley, I saw what was rare in those days, a seagull
come swooping down along the wind. I was fourteen or
thereabouts. With the sight there rose in my mind, as an
automatic expression of what I felt, the following rhymes.
They have their absurdities, of course, but they show that
the flow was there.

> Across the sunlit downs the west wind sings
>   Its ocean melodies, I stand and see
> You wheel the white flash of your long, swift wings
>   And for this moment being I am free:
> As one who holds a shell against his ear
>   And listens rapt until the sullen roar
> Seems in his soul to echo faint and clear
>   The slow surf-murmur of a distant shore.

Memory, of course, was working overtime. I have heard
somewhere else of a man who held a shell to his ear, and 'for
this moment being' is no more than a filler, like 'as of this
moment in time'! Yet the flow was there.

I knew, even then, how strong in me would be the
impulse to rewrite in an inferior manner the more accessible
romantics. Uneasily I wrote my seagull lines down – not
daring to alter a word – I have not done so now – although I
understood their imperfection. Uneasily as time passed and
I fiddled with my two word phrases – my units – I saw the
encouragement of my contemporaries move farther and

287

farther away from what was important to me. I had no
interest in politics, none in the USSR, none whatever in
tractors. I felt the whole generous movement was wrong but
knew that I could not be right. One solitary adolescent! And
yet –

The trouble, of course, was Tennyson. I devoured him
and had done so right back to the time when as a seven-
year-old I had taken home 'hafaleeg hafaleeg hafaleegonward'
as some wonderful stuff the seniors had learned. As an
adolescent I fell for *splendour falls* and *willows whiten* and
now sleeps the crimson petal. Only *Come down O maid from
yonder mountain height* troubled me. I knew the poem faced
the wrong way for all its verbal magnificence – I knew that
even if someone could not *glide a meteor by the blasted pine*
he should not pesuade someone else from that height or let
on he could not reach it himself. Besides, Tennyson, I knew,
was 'out'. As a child, boy, adolescent, young man, I still
loved him in the face of all criticism. I knew his deficiencies.
It will be a bleak world when we love nothing but perfection.
I could understand Tennyson, readily enough, since after a
brilliant boyhood he never again got his intellectual feet wet.
He was wholly accessible. He was a master of the phrase but
spread his thought nearly as thin as Swinburne did. His
stance was more rigid even than mine. His instinct was to
keep things as they were. In a word, he was 'bourgeois',
which as much as anything else was why he was 'out'. I was
not to know how often he would be in and out during my
lifetime.

Like Tennyson I lacked intellectual mobility, or if I had
any intellect and mobility I was too lazy to use it. I went on
writing my sub-Thomas, sub-Keats verses. I fashioned them
as if from precious metal. The eloquence of immediacy
appeared less and less often. It came sometimes in moments
of savage contempt, as when I heard people lusting after
murder cases and executions. I acquired a mass of odds and
ends in the way of verse. I moved from school to university,

still young for my age and ineffably naïve. The flow seemed heavily blocked.

Yet there was a pressure somewhere. I can be sure of that because of an experience analogous to the one with the seagull which I only now recall in mind after a lapse of exactly fifty years. In my first year at Oxford I met a man who dabbled in hypnotism. I was eager for any experience that would release me from an increasingly grey daylight and from the labs where the frogs twitched and the rabbits' guts swelled in the hot summer humidity. I embraced his proposal that he should hypnotize me and he made his passes. I knew it was no good but pretended in a curious way which I think must apply to all subjects under hypnotism – a co-operation and a pretence that was only half a pretence. When the light of the room became normal again I saw that my acquaintance was looking pale. I raised my eyebrows at him. He wiped his forehead with a handkerchief which I remember was rather dirty. 'It was like a chapter of the Old Testament.'

I never saw him again.

A friend lent me a typewriter. Another sent a sheaf of my verses to the publisher. They were not the ones I would have chosen, merely those to hand which I had already typed. I received a letter from a Captain Macmillan offering me five pounds and a place among my contemporaries, Yvonne ffrench, Hugh MacDiarmid, T.W. Ramsey, R.C. Trevelyan, Norman C. Yendell. I kept the secret and waited for the day of publication, like Peacock's Mr Scythrop, and like Scythrop was disappointed for, of course, nothing happened. My experience was that of tens of thousands of other would-be poets. I sent off a second collection of verses written since the others, including many that had missed the first volume, but Captain Macmillan was no longer interested. He may well have been right.

Rosamond Lehmann

THE SOCIETY OF AUTHORS, to whom I have been deeply indebted for wellnigh half a century, has invited me to contribute to this series; so I am delighted to comply, although the effort of looking back so far still wakes an echo of that nervous shrinking which affected me in the mid-twenties when, almost overnight, I burst upon the contemporary literary scene with the publication of *Dusty Answer*.

It seems another life – irrecapturable except in fragments. My sheltered, privileged youth-time must have prevented me from coming to grips with reality in a number of ways. I had never left home until at the age of seventeen I went to Girton College, Cambridge. During those three academic years my fixed conviction that I was destined to be an author, preferably a poet, suffered some sharp and humiliating reverses. The stream of words that had once flowed with such facility dwindled and dried up. The Great War was just over; food was still scarce and horrible; the mood of Cambridge – so far as a ludicrously segregated and chaperoned existence enabled one to test it – was dislocated, feverish and rather sombre – not carefree anyway. Where did I fit in? In those days girls of my particular walk in life did not look for jobs, or embark without hesitation on a professional career. Teaching? – yes, but it had never occurred to me to earn my living by becoming a schoolmistress – the very thought was anathema to me. Marriage? – well, marriage *of course*; but I had it lodged in my subconscious mind that the wonderful unknown young man whom I should have married had been killed in France, along with all the other wonderful young men; so that any other suitor – and quite a few uprose – would be a secondary substitute, a kind of simulacrum.

I left my student days with a good degree but in confusion and emotional disarray, feeling myself a *manqué* figure, but still voicing my determination to be a novelist. Yet how could I become one, I asked in a bitter moment, without some experience of life beyond the bounds of home – where I was 'needed' owing to my father's sadly declining health? My mother pointed out that the Brontë girls had managed it, and I was silenced. But I see now – or think I see – that she was wrong. They were, all three of them, forced at one time or another, to leave home, and it was the anguish of that wrenching, of being torn from that uniquely nurturing womb of Haworth Parsonage, that was for each of them so catastrophic and creative.

After a year or so I married and went to live in Newcastle-upon-Tyne. It was then that the problems of identity and meaning started to become acute. Outwardly I was an enviable, popular young woman, married into a distinguished (teetotal) family, mistress of a large solid house in a Victorian terrace, and (good heavens!) of a cook and a house-parlour-maid, enthusiastic tennis player, giver of somewhat joyless little dinner parties (no wine, no spirits – it appals me to remember); and no prospect of a pram in the hall.

Like Wordsworth's Ruth, I was sick for home – not for my actual home, but for a different gentler landscape, other modes of thinking, feeling, future-building. I was assailed by blank misgivings. I was a misfit – I wanted to desert. I started to write a novel, envisaging this vaguely as an escape hatch. After a few feeble chapters, I tore them up. Then, suddenly, a deeper level of consciousness seemed to open up. I wrote rapidly, with extreme diligence, with scarcely an erasure. 'A woman's principal work', says dear Mrs Gaskell, 'is hardly left to her own choice; nor can she drop the domestic charges devolving on her for the most splendid talents that ever were bestowed.' But although Mrs Gaskell was – and still is – one of my heroines, I cast away her precepts. I left Newcastle and retired to lodgings on the Dorset coast, finished the book, recopied it in my best longhand, and returned with a sense of secret exhilaration.

That summer I met George Rylands (Dadie) for the first time. I asked him to read a novel I had written. Nobly he consented; even more nobly offered to send it to (Sir) Harold Raymond of Chatto & Windus, with a note of recommendation. Less than a month later came the un-believable, the thrilling news: I was thought promising enough to be accepted, published. I was about to become an author!

After that, and until the day of publication, I lived in a state of mingled apprehension and high expectation. The rest I have told elsewhere, and can only condense and recapitulate. Critics in those days were apt to be, if less sharp or downright rude, more moralistic and censorious. The first couple of reviews I saw gave the impression that I had gravely offended against standards of womanly decorum. I wished the earth to open and swallow me up. How could I have unwittingly overstepped the mark? Had I written too frankly on unhealthy subjects such as sexual love and passion? Was there not a hint somewhere of something ambiguous, unmentionable? My loyal mother was startled and distressed. There was talk among elderly relatives and neighbours. One wrote to say that there was alas! a lot of unpleasantness in the world, but why write about it?

But then, after that first upsetting week, a long article by Alfred Noyes, God bless him, appeared in *The Sunday Times*. If Keats were alive today, it said, he might have written such a novel. And all at once, bewilderingly, the book took off, had rave notices, became a bestseller. Book of the month in the USA. Translated into most European languages. In France the object of a kind of cult. And letters, letters, literally hundreds, poured in from strangers: mostly fan letters from young women, but once or twice venomous, abusive, such as one signed 'Mother of Six' and containing a simple message: 'Before consigning your book to flames, would wish to inform you of my disgust that anyone should pen such filth, especially a MISS.'

It does seem strange in retrospect that this romantic, over-emotional but surely innocent work should have aroused such extravagances of response. It must have been one of those inexplicable explosions of the *Zeitgeist*. As for me, it would be less than true to pretend that I did not experience pleasure, gratification, from my sudden change of status. But my overall recollection is of agitation, qualms. Like the old woman in the nursery rhyme I wanted to exclaim: *'This is none of I!* Don't read me. Read somebody else.' And I began to hate my central protagonist – one of my sub-selves I suppose (to borrow a phrase from Elizabeth Bowen) embarrassingly vulnerable, self-absorbed, glamorized.

It is all a long time ago. I think that when the commotion had died down, the consensus of informed opinion, certainly among the highbrow pundits, was that I had written my autobiography, and would never be heard of again.

But I hadn't. And I was.

THE DEFINITE MAYBE

Tom Stoppard

EVERY NEW PLAY is old. No, that's going too far, but there is a marketing problem involved, a time-lag between writing and production which is a serious matter for a new writer, because the younger he is, the faster he is learning and changing. And not just writers, of course: as the Beatle said, mournfully plugging the latest LP, 'I don't know – it was all so long ago, we're doing something different now.' That's probably how most playwrights feel by the time the curtain goes up:

> I had intended this to be
> My next first night but three . . .

I started writing a play some eight years ago. But someone told me that it could take 'anything up to two years to get put on, if it's worth putting on at all', so it hardly seemed worth bothering; I was already late as it was, two years late if you start counting from Osborne'. . . .

However, in July 1960, sitting gloomily in the turquoise sea, waiting for the mainland boat to rescue me from the crush of Capri, I remembered that it was my twenty-third birthday; twenty-three and still unpublished, still unstaged – still, as a matter of fact, un-writing, and two more years

---

[1] John Osborne's *Look Back in Anger* was first staged at the Royal Court Theatre on 8 May 1956.

behind my schedule (horrors! – two more, and I shall have to wear the bottoms of my trousers rolled). So getting back to Bristol from my annual three weeks, I handed in my notice after six years of reporting, subbing, reviewing and inter-viewing and, having contracted to write two weekly columns for a total of six guineas, started writing a stage play, *A Walk on the Water*.

My first play was supposed to have been for the *Observer*'s competition in 1958, but that one petered out after a dozen pages that were not unlike *Look Back in Anger*. This one was not unlike *Flowering Cherry*. I took it round to the Bristol Old Vic. Nothing happened for nine months. I wrote seventy-two more columns, and a one-acter not unlike *Waiting for Godot*.

Of course, another writer would not have waited that long. He would at least have revolted against the sheer inefficiency, or the discourtesy of letting nine months go by without a yes, no, or maybe. But I was diffident about *A Walk on the Water* and, anyway, it was obvious to me that my name would be made by the one-acter as soon as someone read it. At the end of 1961 I sent the latter to an agent, who liked it enough to ask if I'd got anything else for him to see. With misgivings and deprecating noises, I sent him *A Walk on the Water*, explaining that it was, of course, rather *passé* compared to the one-acter, but. . .

Before the week was out I had been summoned to London amid great excitement. An option was bought almost immediately and, drunk with riches (£100), I went out and bought books and a Picasso print. A few weeks later the option had passed to H.M. Tennents, and April (1962) seemed a likely date for the opening. Because it was not unlike *Flowering Cherry* it was sent to Ralph Richardson, who declined it on the grounds that it was not unlike *Flowering Cherry*. There was also talk of Sir Alec. And what did I think of Leo McKern? A year later the option ran out and was not renewed.

At the end of 1963 *A Walk on the Water*, adapted, was televised, a day or two after the Kennedy assassination. ('Jolly bad luck,' said Rediffusion.)

At about that time, my agent picked up my interest in Rosencrantz and Guildenstern and suggested a comedy about what happened to them in England. For good measure, he added that the King of England might be Lear. The possibility appealed to me and I began work on a burlesque Shakespeare farce. By the autumn of 1964 I had written a bad one, but had got interested in the characters as existential immortals. I scrapped the play and in October 1964 started *Rosencrantz and Guildenstern are Dead*, set not in England but within the framework of *Hamlet*. Jeremy Brooks at the Royal Shakespeare Company heard about it and asked for it, and I sent him two completed acts in April 1965. A few weeks later, amid much reported enthusiasm, the RSC commissioned the third act.

There was a prospect of the play going into the repertoire very soon to replace a drop-out, but the third act written under this pressure was not liked so well. Still, there was talk of a revised version going in back-to-back with Peter Hall's *Hamlet*. After a year, in June 1966, the option ran out.

The previous March, a new production company, Albion Players, who had set up shop and started canvassing for scripts, were sent *A Walk on the Water*. Amid great enthusiasm, an option was bought. Peter Sellers was sounded out. Danny Kaye was mentioned. I started rewriting.

Meanwhile, *Rosencrantz and Guildenstern are Dead* had reached the Oxford Theatre Group, via Frank Hauser, and, revised, was performed at Edinburgh in August. Rave from Bryden[2], telegram from Tynan,[3] and another option with a production, probably in October, at the National Theatre. I

---

[2] Ronald Bryden was drama critic of the *Observer*.
[3] Kenneth Tynan was then Literary Manager of the National Theatre Company.

didn't believe a word of it. But then the cogs inexplicably went into reverse and the production was brought forward to April. I think it *may* just possibly happen – the director came round yesterday with his suggested cuts, so something must be happening.

Back at the ranch, I finished my third rewrite of *A Walk on the Water*, plus new title, three months ago and haven't heard anything since. The option runs out about the time you are reading this.

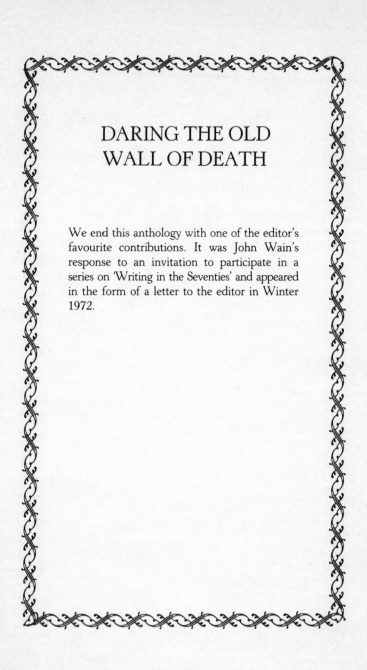

DARING THE OLD
WALL OF DEATH

We end this anthology with one of the editor's favourite contributions. It was John Wain's response to an invitation to participate in a series on 'Writing in the Seventies' and appeared in the form of a letter to the editor in Winter 1972.

Some writers thrive by contact with the commerce of success; others are corrupted by it. Perhaps, like losing one's virginity, it is not as bad (or as good) as one feared it was going to be.

V.S. Pritchett, in a symposium on
'Authors and Advertisement', Autumn 1945

NOT A PROFESSION BUT A CONDITION

John Wain

IN OCTOBER CAME your gentle reminder that the deadline was looming up. And somehow, I still couldn't get the cover off the typewriter. I thought about it, in odd moments, as I have been doing since mid-summer, but there was nothing I particularly wanted to say. I mean, there were lots of things that struck me as reasonably relevant, but no one thing that I wanted to say, to an audience of my fellow writers and their associated publishers, booksellers and librarians, more than any other thing.

Now, on just about the last day, with the post leaving in an hour, I must sit down at last and write, not an article but a letter to you, explaining why I can't write the article after all.

It seemed so simple. A few facts, a few impressions, a few words of comradely encouragement to people who, whatever their differences, are in the same business and have the same problems: who could grudge the time to so worthy a paper?

That, in fact, is insoluble problem number one. *The Author* is worthy: serious, unblinking, down to earth. As the only trade paper we writers have, and as the organ of the only society that looks after our interests, its duty is to face facts, and that's why I never read it. I have tried a few times, but the result of reading through an issue has always been to plunge me into a black depression in which I could almost slash my wrists. Facing facts is just what I don't want to do: not those facts, anyway, not the economic and social facts of being a writer.

301

Let me break in with a small, symbolic note. Since I started writing this letter, the margin-spacing device on my typewriter, the little what's-it that stops the carriage in the right position when you move it back to begin a fresh line, has packed up. If the rest of the letter is unevenly spaced on the left-hand side as well as the right, that's the reason. I could of course send it to my typing agency to get it copied beautifully, but there isn't time, and anway they have just put up their prices. It now costs sixty-five pence per thousand words – you Londoners probably think that cheap, but in the provinces we call that a lot of money, and you wouldn't want me to spend that much, would you? The machine will now have to join the three others, yes, *three*, that I have waiting to go to be repaired. The repair shop is in a place where you can't park a car for miles, so it's half a morning's work to go there and to go again and collect the finished job. I shall shirk it for a bit yet. I have five typewriters, and not till four of them have gone u.s. shall I face going to the repair shop. Then my tax inspector will wonder why I suddenly slap in a colossal bill for typewriter repairs. He'll wonder if I'm going into the used typewriter business. End of parenthesis.

Face facts? I want to, yet – the facts of politics, of ecology, of human relationships, of history, of language and literature and philosophy, as many of them as I can take in; even the 'facts of life', about father squirrel and what he gets up to with mother squirrel, a category of information which my fellow writers are trying hard to see I don't go short of. But the facts of my own professional life? The *facts* about how a writer earns his living? Let me be honest. I've stayed in business as a freelance writer for, well, bless us, it'll be coming up to twenty years soon, and I've done it by not facing facts. By living from hand to mouth. By deliberately taking no notice of the wolf at the door and hoping that he'll go away.

I have a fair-sized family to support, my health is no great

302

shakes, I haven't a penny of private income of any kind, I own no property. I have saved no money, I have made no provision for my old age. By the standards of ordinary middle-class life I am, at forty-seven, a failure. Imagine a bank manager or doctor who, at my time of life, had such a record! Yet the fact is that I don't *feel* like a failure. I think, amazingly enough, that I haven't done so badly. In those nearly twenty years, I may have been forced to overproduce; I may have written hundreds of articles and general odds and ends, as well as the shelf-full of books that represent my 'real' work, and some of them may have been pretty thin. But then I think, on the other hand, of the things I *haven't* done. I haven't written any pornography, or crime thrillers, or scripted any trashy films or television series, and as a critic I've never printed an opinion that I didn't whole-heartedly believe was true. All of which makes me holy? Certainly not. But I feel a solid satisfaction at the fact that, whether or not I've made any money, I have at least spent the last twenty years in activity that has done no one any harm and may conceivably have done a few people some good (interested them, opened their eyes to things they hadn't noticed, enriched their thinking and feeling a little bit). And without ministering to any of the tendencies that cheapen and darken our world. The big power-hungry forces, from ideologies to big businesses, have got where they are without any help from me.

And, since you can't keep politics out of anything these days, I have to add that I feel, all the time, a great sense of gratitude that fate decreed I should be a citizen of a liberal democracy, not afraid to select my own subjects to write about and write about them in my own way. In my worst moments, I've never had to face the possibility that Whitehall may suddenly order my arrest because I don't take the correct official line. And the writers and publishers who weary us with their petulant protests about 'censorship', meaning any attempt to restrain them from piling obscenity on obscenity, ought to sit down in a room by themselves and imagine for one hour the life of Pasternak or Solzhenitsyn.

But facts, no. It's like the old Wall of Death – a writer keeps up on the wall by pressing on at full speed and deliberately defying gravity. I want other people to face facts on my behalf, of course – I want *The Author* to go on, and I shall keep up my subscription to the Society. And I hope no one will tell me that by refusing to face economic realities I'm 'letting down my profession'. Lord love you, being a writer isn't a profession – it's a condition.